A PHILOSOPHY OF ANXIETY

A PHILOSOPHY OF ANXIETY

MICHAEL GRANDONE

Copyright © 2023 by Michael Grandone

All rights reserved. No part of this book may be reproduced in any manner whatsoever without written permission except in the case of brief quotations embodied in critical articles and reviews.

First Printing, 2023

Contents

Preface vii

Chapter 1 1

Chapter 2 20

Chapter 3 48

Chapter 4 65

Chapter 5 84

Chapter 6 105

Chapter 7 116

Conclusion 145

Preface

When writing, you are forced to have a voice, and when you are communicating ideas, it is best to be confident in that voice. That was the biggest surprise, and challenge, in writing *A Philosophy of Anxiety*. For things that I know so intimately, I realized how unsure I felt speaking on them. This is the nature of anxiety, though. Being anxious means doubting yourself, the world, and everything in between.

Speaking definitively about anxiety is likely impossible, anyways. Anxiety, like death, is always our own. We can never fully know anyone else's anxiety, and even our own is not easily explained. I cannot make a simple statement like, "Anxiety is red." At best, I could say, "My anxiety is red." But even that metaphor shows the trouble in explaining something like anxiety. It is not red–it does not have a color. I cannot see, hear, smell, taste, or touch anxiety. It is easy to see how you can fall into the trap of dealing with its manifesting, tangible symptoms and not anxiety itself. If you have ever been to therapy, you have probably felt like you were only picking at the effects.

All of this is to say, even in my most confident voice, I feel that I must pay my respects to my hesitations. I do not come offering the undeniable truth. I come offering a possibility, found during my own meditations and consolidations of thoughts, with anxiety.

I offer a perspective, the same as any other philosophy offers. We have already said so much about so many things. We have millennia of philosophical thought, with each century offering its own unique and novel answers to the same questions that have habitually plagued us. And we keep going. We always look to answer the same questions, as if they are never settled. It could be that they never can be. Or it may be that they are so large and so difficult to describe with our language that attacking from different angles, with some successes and some failures, is the only way that we get closer to describing what is truly indescribable in the terms that we seek to describe them.

The old parable of blind men describing an elephant is what I am trying to articulate here. There are many ways to explain the way that we feel, the way that we think, and the way that we live, even when our view may be incomplete. Who am I to say which are right and which are wrong? Which are valuable and which are worthless? And who am I to say where each attempt fails? But it is my perspective which I wish to talk about.

Every meditation on anxiety is a variation on the theme. Anxiety is with us intimately, but we never know it fully. We only ever know our own anxiety, yet we recognize it in others. Anxiety is surprising—no matter how familiar we are with it, it appears out of the darkness in places and ways that we did not expect. But anxiety is not a stranger. Even in the quiet dark, we are confident enough to know it is there, even when it does not announce itself.

Chapter 1

1.1 Anxiety Does Not Make Sense

Something does not feel right. That is how it begins: with that thought. The shaking, the nausea, the headaches, the exhaustion, the terror of the whatever—it all comes later.

I remember not feeling right more than once before it became Anxiety, and before I knew it was something more than a funny feeling. I remember swimming out into a lake, realizing I could not stand on the bottom and keep my head above water. I remember hiking in the mountains, when the realization came over me that if I were to become injured or too fatigued to continue on, I could not make it back to camp. I remember riding in my car and my stomach rumbling as the miles rolled underneath me.

The panic attacks followed. Eventually the feeling stayed. It did not go away when I found solid ground. Like being so high that I had to grip the railing, except I never made it low enough to feel comfortable enough to let go. This is my anxiety. This is my constant fear.

I wake up and wonder if this is it. I am constantly reminded of time gone by. I think of the future, and I become nauseous. I ask myself where it went wrong.

Eventually, it never feels right. That unease tires you out, but keeps you from sleeping. It makes you want to shift your focus, but it demands all of your attention. It consumes you. When there is nothing left, it takes even that nothingness. Anxiety is these contradictions. It does not make sense. Meaning disappears.

1.2 What Anxiety Asks Us

Anxiety is not something that you have to experience. A person does not have to have a panic attack as a response to a stressful situation. It is not essential that someone be nervous to leave the house. No one has to feel nervous before speaking in public. The dread you feel when thinking about your place in life is not necessary. But, it feels like an inevitability.

How is someone supposed to live with anxiety? Even when they are not having a full blown anxiety attack, they worry that they may. Although angst is not full blown in every moment of the day, the malaise affects everything. Every action taken by the anxious person is influenced by their condition. They have to go to an appointment the next day, they eat less for fear of getting sick. They have dinner plans, they drive themselves for fear of being stuck there with no way home. They fear rejection, so they lash out before someone else can.

Anxiety asks you to bend to it, even when you cannot bend anymore. It is something in the way, an obstacle in the mind. But anxiety is not something that appears from somewhere else. Whatever triggers it, anxiety very definitely comes from the inside. It is not an intruding virus, or a burn from an open flame. Your mind, as a part and a propeller of your body, is acting. We acquiesce. We simply do not want to be anxious—and who can blame us? Anxiety and depression do not fit in our world. Best to react to it, as quickly and easily as possible, as it insists. Ignoring it is not a sustainable option.

The inevitable Anxiety demands to be seen. The stress stops me in my tracks. It is there that I meet an entire world, shaded by dread. The new world comes at me there. You could say it was lingering in the woods around me, but it is not just a creature lurking, like a grinning wolf. It is the woods itself. The trees, ready to fold down over me

1.3: Why Fight Anxiety?

A person can go through years of therapy, medication, meditation, suffering, and trying to find answers. They may never ask: why try to conquer anxiety? Assuming they can feed, clothe, and house themself, what benefit is there to that natural response to just beat it down, and get things back to the way that they were?

A person should not resign themself to feeling anxious all of the time, although to be fair, normalizing it is part of the playbook that therapy has one go through. No, the question is really: should they have to engage with their anxiety? Certain activities, certain circumstances, and certain conditions in life can give someone anxiety. Why not cut out those conditions? The focus is almost exclusively on maintaining the status quo and reducing stress around it, maintaining the world and context around them.

But does a person really need the social events? Are the cross-country flights necessary? If someone does not want to leave the house, why should they not just stay home? Life goes on. They continue to exist. Why should they torture themself? If the avoidance is not hurting them or anyone else, why is it not the right course of action?

This is more difficult as the anxiety and depression become larger and more abstract. However, we can still ask: if someone feels generally anxious, existentially even, why is it the anxiety itself that they try to crush? Is anxiety, which does not exist anywhere else except as a type of notion in their own mind, a thing to be rid of?

1.4: Why Not Never?

Why not just never fly? Why not always take the

stairs, never the elevator? Why not never leave the house? Why not ignore your parents?

Take these questions seriously. If a person does not have to fly, and it would give them anxiety to do so, why not just drive when they have to travel? If someone does not like elevators, why not just take the stairs every time they need to climb floors?

It is not as far-fetched as it sounds. There is nothing in it for someone to fly in an airplane for the sake of flying. Other options exist, and they could reasonably plan to use them. There is nothing in the world that says that a person needs to make it from one side of the country to the other in a single morning. If you are afraid of dogs, do not adopt one. Feel free to walk to the other side of the street when there is one chained up in front of a house on your route.

People experiencing anxiety as the result of a specific traumatic experience are often asked to expose themselves to a similar situation, or relive it in other ways. The purpose is to desensitize and recontextualize, and to find a way to endure the tension. It is fair to question these methods.

I have generalized anxiety with a panic disorder. I am definitely agoraphobic to a not insignificant degree. I do not mind being in my backyard, but going to places away from my house is a different story. Being the passenger in a car is not pleasant for me, likely because of a control issue. I am not a great swimmer, and as such, I do not like water that is over my head, whether I am in the water or on a boat on the water.

Eating is treacherous for me. I am afraid of throwing up, and my stomach is constantly upset. This makes eating out, and any social event or interaction, a situation filled with dread. This physical piece contributes to most of the above anxieties, part of an endless loop of anxious feeling both physical and emotional. These are the more tangible expressions of my anxiety. Looking out over my life, behind and in front, the anxiety crawls as well. It is an anxious condition I live in, through and through.

So, as I sit and feel the weight of a stone move through my abdomen, the baseline physical existence of my anxiety, while engine oil soaks my brain and controls the fits and starts of my thinking, and a feeling of faintness is in every muscle of my body, I have to wonder why I am fighting it all so hard. If I do not have to confront things that trigger my anxiety, why do I obsess over it? And why is so much of the treatment for anxiety obsessed with getting us back in the grind, with salvaging the day-to-day?

To be clear, I know there are some times when I cannot avoid it. But what are those times? If I do not want to fulfill an "obligation," must I? Social mores as ruling factors over how we act and how we treat anxiety should be questioned. Adherence to cultural norms need to be broken down, and instead we should be reoriented to what we, as the person at the center of our own worlds, want and need.

Without these artificial ropes, what are we tied to?

1.5: Self-Indulgence

There is nothing new to say. Nothing new has been discovered about anxiety in a long time, and the same things are being re-stated in different ways. Perhaps each iteration is just more contemporary.

The Greeks are quoted by the Romans and the Romans are quoted by the Scholastics, and the Scholastics are quoted by the Renaissance Men, and the Renaissance Men are quoted by the Enlightened and on and on, and people are still sitting sad and anxious and angry and scared. The Scientific Method birthed by this succession lives on, applying to more and more, including our own thoughts.

The journey is through their books. It is listening to their thoughts. If it were easy enough to climb out of the cave, everyone would, because as anybody with anxiety knows, it is not a place that one wants to stay, no matter how accustomed one becomes to headaches, the negative thoughts, and the disappointment.

This examination does not care about the path that it is supposed to take. The past routes have taken us only up to a point. Yet, what more can there be to say on the matter? This is an update to the language–*at best*. The journey is into the question: why must someone overcome anxiety? Put a different way: why does someone have to master the situations that produce anxiety in them, as is the urging of psychological and cultural norms? Why can they not engage with the world that makes them anxious, or not engage, as they please? Why do they have to change themself into something that they do not want?

There is no grand plan to this process. It is a search for any kind of sense or guiding principles, to see if not having anxiety is not only possible, but desirable. Everyone searches themselves when faced with these challenges. Many times, they find some temporary panaceas or axioms to help relieve the pressure. Permanent fixes are hard to find–do they even exist? If they do not, why not? If there is a reason why not, what does that say?

The history of Western thought and society leads to rationality. The Scientific Method is unimpeachable. Data rules. Everything makes sense.

But what happens when reason meets the unreasonable? Anxiety does not conform. It does not spring forth as expected. It is like a glitch in life with how it interrupts, but different in how it does not simply come into and out of existence in a moment. When the rational is confronted with what does not make sense, why does the irrational seem to win?

1.6: You Know How It Goes

Much of the writing about anxiety and depression today does these things:

Hedge. The authors cannot be blamed for doing this. This is not stuff that exists in black-and-white, and your own personal mileage may vary. But the aversion to taking a position and plowing head first with it is dismaying. Sure, someone may discover something new next year or figure something out from a perspective that was never thought of before in a new study or introspection. I am coming from the perspective that committing to my thinking will produce overall positive results, though. I will surely be hedging when it feels like my personal experience is doing an exceptionally large share of the informing of a position—but that is not going to stop me.

Make many faceted arguments. Related to many things not being black-and-white, it can be understood why a spoked book makes sense. Too often, though, the pieces are all slightly linked. They are lists, essentially, with components that are related by the central topic of the story, but with each other, their ties are less joined. If you look at a stained glass window, which section is of more importance: the pieces that make up the background or those of the saint? All of the glass keeps the elements out. Some are more than that.

Reticence to criticize an approach. Someone should not be discouraged from using the approach that works best for them. By all means, whatever gets you through the day. The tradition that some of these ideas and methods come from are deeply flawed, though. Their implications are alarming as well. Not everything is bad and not everything is good. Someone should not be afraid to challenge any approach because there is not an authoritative one.

Walk down cultural memory lane. Our history is too interesting not to be considered. It is also so intertwined in conversations both internal and external that it is hard to avoid it. But by the same token, starting with the etymology of a word ("anxiety comes from the Latin via the French...") can be historically instructive, but tells me little about my nausea.

Situates amongst the greats. Like the above historical trip, the people one meets along the way are always present. Their resilience is a testament to the fact that we really have not moved too far beyond what any of our precursors have to say. We discover something new on every reading.

Get to the how, only to reach hope in the end. It is pretty predictable at this point. So much so that "hope" has become a trope in all of the literature. Here is a fact: there is no preordination of making it out, as if anxiousness is a place.

Recount a conversation with some else, usually their therapist. That is almost like telling someone about your dreams, which nobody cares about, unless you dreamt about them.

1.7: "Why Do I Have Anxiety?"

I have asked why I have anxiety for so long, I forget why I even want to know. Knowing why seemingly normal things, things in the past, and even existence itself, produce such agony does not do any good. Consider those who have suffered trauma. Knowing that trauma does not ease their fears. Do not ask why we have to suffer with the unsureness, the shaking in our bones, jolt of energy from eyes open to eyes close, the flames that exist on the other side of the door that we know are there, without actually looking to see that they are there.

Question how we engage with our anxiety. Does the approach to relieve it make sense? Are we being honest when we try to examine our fears? Are our efforts to move beyond anxiety actually effective and truly treating the anxiety, or are they just efforts to get us through the day? How does the world around us contribute to our anxieties, and can we ever rid ourselves of them in this world?

Is our anxiety trying to tell us something? Can we understand what is being said? Do we want to understand what is said?

Anxiety is speaking to us. It is not just telling us something about ourselves. It is also telling us something about the world around us. Anxiety and depression do not exist in a void. It exists in us, and we are not voids. We are living in a world, shaped by a society that was launched forwards before we, individually, were even here. It is a world with a significance that we are born into.

Everything has a weight. The weight is a force, pushing down on the ground below it. The ground gives back its own force, a "normal force", that holds a thing in place. It prevents weight from overpowering or moving through the surface. We understand that in regular terms: the world is the ground and our weight stands on it. But in the universe of our minds, we are the ground, and it is the weight of the world that is pushing down on us. Why does it feel so heavy sometimes? How are we able to even hold it up? And why not just let it crush us underneath it, eventually passing through until it emerges out the other side, and we are left scattered into the boundless nothingness of the universe, in so many pieces that we become indistinguishable from the nothing? What would it have been for Atlas to have crumbled underneath the weight of the cosmos?

The weight that pushes down on the world is also bestowed by it. Gravity, mass, matter–physical things –are literally of the physical world and the universe. In our flipped metaphor, the irony exists: the weight of the world that we experience, bearing down on us and stimulating anxiety, is given by our own minds. When something gets heavy, and it is harder to carry than it was when we first picked it up, it has not gained weight. Our ability to lift it has changed. Anxiety wears on the mind the same way

Fortunately, fears and anxious thoughts do not have actual mass, and they are not made of matter. The physical world does not bind us to being crushed by the psychic one. Dropping it will not destroy us. Dropping it is not a certainty either–nor is downward momentum.

1.8: There Is a Script

There is a script. *This is what you do when you have anxiety: Make these phone calls. Do these exercises. Take this stuff. Read these books. This is how you are supposed to react to it.*

But why is that what someone is supposed to do? How effective is it at relieving anxiety and depression? What are the results?

The doctors are called. Breathing techniques and exercises are practiced. Maybe there are vitamins to take and food to eat that will help. Certainly there are pills. Search on "anxiety" and "depression" and there are an immeasurable number of self-help manuals and workbooks. These are all the things that one does to beat anxiety back, to put it behind them, where they do not have to hear from it ever again, so that the alarm clock can go off in the morning, waking them up from sleep because they had not been laying there panicking for hours already, and they can get out of bed and be on with their daily routines. Cannot be late. Or miss that appointment.

If every day they are going back through this choreography, how well is it working? If this is the work that it takes to make it through their day, it is no wonder they are exhausted by the end of it, which is some ironic sweet relief because it may help them fall asleep. Except, of course, they wake up before the sun, because the sleep is enough rest to allow them to function, but not enough to escape the unease that keeps their mind restless. The push of the dismay overtakes the pull of fatigue. That is not to say that the fatigue goes away, as again, running through this script is exhausting on its own. Keeping it together is a slog.

Are people supposed to shudder at the appearance of anxiety? Bury their heads in their hands? Go under the covers. Take a mental health day. Then get up the next and go back to work? Call a therapist. Maybe a psychologist. Maybe a psychiatrist. Get some medication. Do yoga. Get back on the bike and go back and forth every day like nothing ever happened?

Or is anxiety a call to change? To excise something.

Some therapies of the past have fallen out of favor or outright abandoned. Institutionalization. Lobotomies. Shock therapy. Bloodletting.

We know to be healthier. Vodka is not a good answer. Exercise helps. Some drugs are back, and some are better than others.

All of it is so that someone can jump right back in. To not lose a step. But maybe anxiety is trying to deliver a message: Something does not *feel* right, because something *is* not right.

1.9: I Know Why

I have always known why I was anxious. I just did not want to upset the order of things, either consciously or subconsciously. It was not that deep down, and it did not take much to dredge it up at first. Every time that I had a panic attack, every time I sat across from a therapist, every time I woke up in the morning and that first shot of cortisol pulsed through my body, I knew why I was anxious. What was in front of me was not how I thought it should be, or how I wanted it to be.

That was my own failing, I said to myself. Where I was—where I am—is because of my own inability to bring myself where I want to go, and where I think I should be. My own inadequacies are to blame, I would think. My own underachievements are responsible for the world I find myself in, or that I will find myself in. My self-assigned purpose was not being fulfilled. I was not surviving the world that I was in, and I would not survive what the world would continue to throw at me.

At least that is how the thinking goes. The triggers may differ. The starting points may change. But it was always because of the self's unrealized potential. I am in this place, when I should be in another place. What is happening is something that should not be happening. A block exists between myself and meaning: the way that it is supposed to be.

This applies at both a macro level, as well as a micro. Someone may not be able to articulate the meaning of their life, but they naturally have a sense of what they are supposed to be doing at a given moment. That could mean that they think that they should have been an astronaut. It could also mean that they think that they should be able to give a speech without stammering.

So it is understandable to some degree how that mindset should be treated as invalid. After all, it certainly reeks of being too harsh on oneself, too judgemental, with too much guilt and remorse over perceived sins for which they feel shame. But what is being absolved?

I feel guilty because I am not working more towards my goals, or because my weak stomach gives me pause when i go to a restaurant, or because I am worried about the social flogging I will take if I do something embarrassing. All of that can be tempered. But why should I be re-wired for the very human feelings that I have? The conversation should not be one-sided.

If the room is cold, sometimes I put on a sweater. Other times, I turn up the heat.

1.10: A Metaphysics of Anxiety

I have asked myself a question at my high points and at my low points. At my best and at my worst. At my lightest and darkest. When everything was great and when I was crushed by the air into the couch cushions and only able to exhale, not inhale. At all of these times, I have never found a cosmic answer to the question: why? Why do I have anxiety? Why am I in this fight? Why fight it? Why beat it?

Answers do not exist.

There is no unified theory of anxiety. Metaphysics

does not explain this. For every axiom, idiom, imperative, moral, or word to live by, the world comes roaring back. It is relentless in its imposition.

But I want the metaphysics. I want them badly. I need more. Meaning and purpose. I crave them. I cannot just be satisfied with this: the symptoms. The nausea. The headaches. The exhaustion. The sleepless nights. The doubts. The anger. The sadness. The funny feeling that something is not right. I am more than this—but what, I do not know. I am more than just materials, chemicals. More than just atoms. More than just my conditioned response. Nature and nurture are both corporeal.

Floating in the ocean, does the shark I am searching for know that I am searching for it? This quest has something at the end, right? Tell me it is findable. The time, the energy, is a cost being paid daily. After all, the search is so much of what it takes to get through the day.

What if I were to give up the search, because what if there is no reason to search? A meaningless search.

1.11: A Philosophy of Anxiety

I believe that there is a way to find a philosophy through anxiety.

But, I want to contend that anxiety does more than tell us about ourselves. It does more than make us question existence. It is more than a reaction to the world that we find ourselves in. Does anxiety tell us how we should live? Is anxiety a guide? Are our aversions to it disordered, and our methods for overcoming it misguided?

Certainly, when it comes to anxiety in the aftermath of a traumatic event, we recognize that the anxiety is justified by past lived experience. The anxiety makes some sense, in a certain respect. Putting your hands on the anxiety and pushing back against it is no less difficult, however my near-drowning correlates to my fear of swimming in water above my head. (As an aside, other people seem to accept these types of anxieties more. They are clear traumas that are culturally understood and agreed to be universally traumatic.)

But what about when the root and the reaction is more ephemeral: when the anxiety is not the scar of an event, or a phobia of something that can be seen or touched? When it is more general, and more all-encompassing, what then? Is it trying to communicate something? It may not be explaining why the anxiety exists, but instead it may be declaring what the reaction to the world should be. Is it saying something about the world, and our lives? And to what extent is that anxious voice really our own voice?

1.12: How Should One Live with Anxiety?

How should someone live, as an anxious person, in an anxious world?

Anxiety is a real reaction to the world. One must react to the world as it comes at them. People obsess over their reaction to the anxiety itself, when in reality their posture towards the world is what needs focus.

Anxiety is a piece of that reaction. Anxiety is a driver of that reaction. Anxiety says that there must be a reaction. The world and the interpretation of it demand that something be done.

Anxiety is a demand to change the way that we live. It is a demand to change our orientation to the world. It is a demand to change the world. It is a world devoid of meaning and caring. It is a world indifferent to us, and the anxiety it causes.

What is our reaction to that indifference? How is our life shaped by it? And how does anxiety press down on it, and on us?

Chapter 2

2.1: Why Bother? (What Prize Exists?)

When anxiety is always present, a feeling of "why bother?" creeps into all thinking.

If you engage with the thing or activity that gives you anxiety, you know that you will become more anxious, possibly panic, and possibly have an attack. So why even court that possibility? Does it make more sense to avoid it, and be able to make it to another day?

We create loops in our heads based on experiences. Some of those loops may include inferences, or ideas that we create. Some may be unreasonable when looked at from a different perspective. But are they totally without merit? Whether the danger that we sense is reasonable or not, the fear is not imaginary. The anxiety and the physical symptoms that manifest are very real, both in the mind and in the body.

What prize exists for making oneself nauseous with distress? Who are we impressing? What salvation are we guaranteeing? Someone can expose themself over and over again, perhaps numbing the pain of anxiety. But to what end? What is truly lost? The world will turn without us.

2.2: Why Bother? (These Are Not New Ideas)

These are not new ideas. They are barely even new words. "Why bother?" is basically, "Why live?" Thinkers of the Existentialist tradition ask this when they contemplate suicide. It was asked before that, too. Even the Ancient Greek father of modern philosophy Socrates, condemned to death, accepted his fate.

We are in a world of anxiety. Our constant condition is anxiousness. It is almost as if being anxious is what it is to be human. We are always presented with things that will not be still within us. Our being rebels. We act out. Or act inwardly, in a way.

So if this condition is omnipresent, why bother? If the weight that we are carrying is not going to lessen, why are we trying to carry more?

2.3 Values Big and Small

Somewhere, someone does not feel like leaving the house today. They do not feel like working today. Someone does not want to wake up early. They do not want to go out to dinner. They do not feel like seeing their family today. They do not feel like going into the city, or into town, to the store, or to the airport. They do not feel like flying on a plane.

At some point, a person has to ask: why must I do these things?

There may be good, necessary reasons sometimes. (For instance, the doctor's office is not a place someone necessarily wants to go to, but the benefit is clear. Nobody wants to go to a funeral, but they find a reason to go.) Other times, many times, the reasons are not there. They would rather be doing something else, or simply not that thing. The actions that people have to do—are supposed to do—may seem necessary to the anxious person, but they do not feel that they are actually necessary in a more profound, meaningful sense.

Replace the banal actions mentioned above with more principled examples. I believe that we should be kind and decent in everyday interactions. I believe that people should act ethically and morally. I believe in charity. I believe that people should not go hungry in a prosperous society.

What happens when your values are not valued by others, or even the opposite of what you believe comes to pass in the world? What happens when I fall short of acting in the way that I think I should act, the way I should be? Or, why does ambivalence creep in?

Decisions are not always as simple as choosing between one of two things, when one is the good option and the other is the bad option. Our ability to choose is not always foolproof either. But certainly, there is what we want and value, and what the world outside of us requires and values.

Why is the world the way that it is? Why is our society this way? Why is our culture shaped like this?

Any why is any of it not the way that I think it should be, the way that I have been taught it is, the way that I have come to believe in it?

Why does a world that is supposed to make sense, not make sense?

2.4: The Feeling Builds

An interesting feature of anxiety is how it can exhibit its own growth. A bit of nervousness as a fleeting thought can become a minute of anxiety. That minute can then be an hour tomorrow. The hour can become an entire waking day of angst. Someone can have uneasy feelings that they feel before going to bed, and wake up the next day with them still there.

This is to say nothing of sleepless nights.

The reasoning that leads to anxiety in one aspect of life has a way of becoming a normal thought process, automatically running, and spreading to other parts. This way of thinking becomes a baseline way of thinking. Everything is based around that anxiety, and the conditions of that anxiety.

A stomach ache in the morning becomes something to take into account for later in the day, for future days, and for life. That anxiety felt today becomes an anxiety that is not only chronic, but *expected* to be chronic. It has grown from a ping to a thought to a mode, being all of these at once, changing the anxious person's life and forever thinking that they have to feel this way for the rest of their existence.

To the anxious person, anxiety has taken what is possible, their ability to imagine, and their future.

2.5: Hard to Get Away from Why

It is hard to get away from the question of "why" I have anxiety. I am constantly searching for the reason. I tell myself: if I knew the reason, I could beat it, and I would not be anxious anymore.

Or maybe it is because I know why I am anxious and depressed, but I never want to confront it. Meanwhile, it is constantly finding me, showing up everywhere I go. It does not follow me, because it is there before I arrive.

Is it me? How much of the anxiety is external and how much is internal? Certainly my mind plays a part. My ability to deal with stressors contributes to the force that the stressors put on me. Some of those stressors are unavoidable to a degree.

But to be anxious is to be constantly presented with this questioning. We, as humans, are constantly trying to make sense of what we feel and what we think. Oftentimes, when the unavoidable or the locked in consequences of our circumstances present us with an explanation, we try to find another, or simply look away, averting our gaze. The truth is too daunting. It is too much to confront. It may represent a mistake that we made in the past. It may clash with our values.

2.6: Experiences as They Are Presented

Anxiety cannot be treated as something entirely of the mind. Changing mindsets is not all there is to overcoming anxiety. Anxiousness is the result of the inability to comprehend and truly accept experiences as they are presented, and as they are interpreted. Each piece–the comprehension, acceptance, interpretation–is not independent. They exist in concert. They rely on each other, as well as something totally outside of them: the world.

If someone's reasoning is faulty, being a rational person should mean that their thinking adjusts to be more true. They may know logically, easily even, that their fears are not sensible. They can tell themself that their fear of heights is not based on any reasonable safety issue or plausible chain of events that could lead to being hurt. But that does not ease anxiety, no matter how adept their internal monologue may be. Reasoning must be filled with content to be effective.

They can accept the situation that they find themself in. but that does not necessarily improve their situation. Accepting that a meteor is headed towards Earth does not put the mind at ease. Open-ended acceptance is also difficult, if not impossible. No, acceptance requires something to accept (to say nothing of the fact that whatever it is, must be acceptable).

Interpretations–the conclusions that someone draws based on the things presented to them–can also be adjusted. If someone is anxious about what other people think of them, and they fret over a reaction that they received, it is possible for them to reconsider it, and conclude that a short answer that they received from a friend was not because they do not enjoy their company, but instead about a piece of distressing news that they received earlier in the day. Would that resolve their general feelings of anxiety around social interactions and situations? It is likely that it would not on its own. Interpretations exist with momentum. They are informed from the outside, even as they kaleidoscope ideas. The kaleidoscope, with its own internal universe, is still turned from the outside.

Finally, if the world itself—what someone experiences—triggers feelings of panic and distress, they can remove pieces to an extent. If someone is afraid of deep water, they can not swim into depth over their heads. Of course, this tactic cannot work for everything. There are obligations that a person may have, or things that they want to do and experience. It should be remembered that these things themselves are not an actual physical source of anxiety. The ocean on its own does not contain anxiety or depression, despite any danger that it may present. A person's understanding, internalization, and rendering play significant parts, even if something like the ocean materially exists. The internal and external all have roles in the experience.

2.7: The Future / Anticipatory Anxieties

We are fortune tellers. And we are not bad at it. I do not have to think about what happens when I press my finger on this keyboard. The letters will appear. When I leave the house to go to the grocery store, the route, the building, the way I find my items and buy them, are all automatic to me. Brushing everyday will lead to reduced problems with my teeth, I expect. As time passes and I grow older, my hair will become greyer. We are prescient in our everyday thoughts and actions.

The future that we tell is a declaration of what we believe *will be,* together with what we think *should be.* We arrive at these two projections informed by our pasts. In the present, we predict the future, using the past. Our experiences and what we observe allow us to imagine what we expect of the future. In a practical sense, our expectations can be very accurate. For instance, we mentally construct the cause and effect of boiling a pot of water. Here, we construct what will be. But that is not always all that we imagine. Sometimes, we construct multiple ideas of what *can be*, weighing each without effort and subconsciously choosing a *will be.* Sometimes we assign less practical, but value-ridden conclusions. This is what we believe *should be.* What *should be* is simple to live with when talking about something tangible, like putting the needle to a record. But it is more fraught when connected to our mental state, our emotional reactions, events that we assign meaning to, and likewise for other people's input into this ecosystem, at least in terms of what we expect. The value assigned with our expectations produces a fuller experience.

There are these futures because without a value-added version, we would be indifferent objects moving through the world, satisfied with where the gravity of the satellites around us push and pull.

We see the multiple futures at once: the *will be* with the *should be* may sometimes be the same. But in the cases where they are at opposite poles of the globe and even irreconcilable, anxiety is found. The future we envision is not the future we think should come to pass.

Consider the experience of someone that has survived a trauma. Driving in a car one night, they were hit by another driver, and fortunately survived, but with significant injuries. After this accident, they experience severe anxiety at the prospect of riding in an automobile again. The past experience of the collision and injury has made an imprint on their thinking. They foresee a future where they *will be* hurt if they ride in the car, and of course that is something that they do not want, and it *should be* avoided. This thought process makes some sense. We know that the likelihood of being in another accident like the previous experience is small, but we also have experienced panic and anxiety ourselves and know that our mind does not weigh scenarios that way.

In a twist that we are all familiar with, the anxiety

(or the anxious reaction) becomes its own experience. Now, the future is filled with anxiety itself in somewhat of a self-fulfilling prophecy. Our soothsaying taps into its own faculties and predicts how its own cause-and-effect thought process will react. The loop is created and the loop continues. The future is foreseen because the future is our function.

2.8: We Do Not Know the Future

Of course, we do not really know the future. There are things that we expect. Things we take for granted will happen. We know what can be. We believe that some things will come to be. We also have ideas of how things should be. But these are not all infallible thoughts.

Unfortunately, with anxiety, we are aware of the fallibility of our thoughts, particularly our positive ones. As anyone that suffers from anxiety and depression will tell you, often what this means is preparing for the worst, or what we think are the worst, outcomes to a debilitating degree. It is a life of bracing oneself to be pushed—and leaning, to be ready to absorb the blow. It is leaning up against a wall so that the shove has nowhere to send you—you are already up against it.

Unsure of our own thinking, and ready for disaster, low self-esteem reigns. Now, this is not to say that if we could accurately predict the future, we would be happier or better off. But, when our imagination is not in this state of play, the state of anxiety overtakes all other modes of thinking.

2.9: Where the Mental Meets the Physical

What comes first? The nausea or the anxiety? In some ways, anxiety feels like a self-fulfilling prophecy. It is anxiety about an experience that can make an experience bad. Depression colors the room before someone enters it, just as in the reverse, someone is colored by the room with their anticipatory thinking.

This all often feels like some kind of dark magic to the anxious. But it is less so than it seems in the thick of it. The brain, and its reasoning function is so good at what it does, it is not only in the state of play solely when we are obsessing over the world around it, but also while it is not aware of it. An algorithm is run in the background, preparing someone for what is to come. The subconscious mind has a head start on the conscious mind. It has the connections, too. To the stomach and to pores. To the lungs, and nerves. The mind itself is part of the physical self, after all.

It is right at this point, where the world outside of us becomes a world inside of us, that what is not the physical self becomes something physical within, and gives birth to anxieties, both consciously and subconsciously.

2.10: Science of Anxiety

I am not anti-Science. Far be it from me to disagree with years of research, study, and established fact. The world is round: I believe that.

But science is not everything, and it is not the end point of human experience. In some respects, theory has taken over for truth. In others, entire aspects of our selves are pushed to the side, as if not relevant enough to be considered a cause or an actor in explaining and addressing the world that we are presented with.

I think about a conversation that I had when I was younger. The person I had it with was probably filled with a youthful exuberance for ideas that we all experience at one time or another (and some never escape). We were on the car ride leg of a trip back from New York to Massachusetts. It was night time, and in the midst of it, we pulled off of the highway for a brief stop. It was at a random exit, the kind where you accidentally turn right from the offramp when you should have turned left, and you have to turn around in a large abandoned parking lot of a school or community center, where nothing is happening beyond the high light poles lighting the pavement.

He was arguing that love was what we called our evolved desire for another person, based on evolutionary needs developed over time, embedded into our biology. So, if I were to find one person more attractive or lovable than another, it would be because on a certain level I found them the best mate for my own preservation.

Now, that has some obvious shortcomings as a theory, and being a good friend I never asked his then long-time partner (who he later went on to happily marry) if she thought their relationship was purely founded on evolutionary bedrock, rather than, say, enjoying each others' company above others. I think about this and wonder: why are anxiety, depression, and other mental health topics treated with a similar, if not identical, textbook adherence to base-level human behavior?

The physical aspects of anxiety are knowable. We can cite fatigue, aching, excitability, irritability, and overall trouble concentrating easily. We can also identify the worrying thoughts, the loop they maintain, and the way that it spirals uncontrollably. The interplay between all of these symptoms either amount to something more, or leave out other aspects of anxiety that are more ethereal.

After all, if it were just exhaustion and negative thoughts, we would be able to treat anxiety like we treat a headache or how we prepare for an exam. Chemical explorations of the brain seek this route as well. These biological factors do contribute to our lives, but in what ratio to the rest of it?

All of the conditions above are knowable. But do they explain anxiety? Can we understand it only in those terms? Is anxiety knowable solely through science and fact? Science tells us it is all explainable, all factual. It is not.

The attempt at defining anxiety is noble. Nobody should be faulted for attempting it. But in approaching anxiety from the couch and the pharmacy counter, the wider reaching undercurrent of both unease and mental terror have been left unaddressed.

Anxiety is not supernatural, though. It is something that is experienced, definitely, in the world. In some ways it is irrational. In others, it is emotional. It is also metaphysical. It permeates our being, even if it is not a condition or pillar of our being.

Treatment, whether human or pharmacological, can help us cross a bridge, and when we do that they will say, "See, you did it!"

"Yes, but it was, and I am, miserable," we reply. There is more than just practical accomplishment of a task or a journey. Overcoming a fear should not just be about the result. How we experience it contributes to our place in the world just as much as the outcome.

In this way, the anxiety exists in the world itself.

Our experience of the world is inextricably intertwined with our interpretation of it. Anxieties have their say in a way that is not measurable with instruments or objective descriptions. Yet their existence and influence is present like any other system of thought and understanding is.

We can try to hold these things in our hands as much as possible, but the only true understanding of it will come in our own experience of it.

2.11: "Anxiety"

If it already is not clear: I am using the word "anxiety" broadly. We have listed the physical symptoms. You know them and live them. But they are particular to you. They are relatable–we all know what sweaty palms are like, even if they are not something that you yourself get when you become nervous. For some it reaches panic attack levels. For others, it turns into a feeling of depression. We know the general shape of these things. But describing it is still like trying to hold water in your hands, or defining any primary color.

No matter how hard I try, no matter my empathy, no matter my education, I cannot know exactly how you experience anxiety. It is difficult enough to describe my own anxiety. How can I explain that it is so hard to get on? As a collection of feelings, both physical and mental, the result is what makes it anxiety. Individually, some of these emotions or pings may not make me anxious, but in conjunction with each other, they become panic. As a metaphor, pretend being anxious has a value of 100. Anxious could be 49 plus 51. It could be 33 plus 20 plus 47. It could be 20 times three minus 10 plus 50. What our individual experiences add up to resemble a shared definition of anxiety.

The intensities may vary. Something that makes us anxious today may not make us anxious tomorrow. Something that makes you anxious obviously does not necessarily make me anxious. The way that we manifest a reaction also differs. Some of us pace. Some stay in bed. Some tap their feet. These are anodyne examples. There are much more destructive behaviors as well. There is violence.

The nature of our own violence varies, and in turn, the multiplicities of it are all unique and personal. Understanding it exactly is impossible. So how do we discuss it?

At base, anxiety is an inner aversion. It is a conscious or unconscious recognition of an incongruity that each of us wishes to contrast or prevent. How we experience that and how we act on it differs.

2.12: This Is Not the Way It Is Supposed to Be

If naturally we want to think through our anxious thoughts, and understand them, we may inevitably reach a place in our minds that is somewhere that we do not want to be, a place we do not recognize, or even nowhere.

When we reason our own lives, harsh thoughts can spring up.

This is not the way it is supposed to be.
This is not going the way it is supposed to go.
This will not be what I want.
This will not be good.

The thoughts are both assessments of our current state and of our future state.

How did I get here? My past experience, upbringing, acuity, codes of living (moral and otherwise), and perhaps even some delusion set expectations. The prism that they construct refracts my context in life, upon which I try to make sense of myself and of the world.

So it may not be that I am actually living in some type of dire straits. But on some level, whether consciously or unconsciously, I see the room that I am in, I look at the events on my calendar, or maybe I daydream about myself growing old, and I become nauseous. And that nausea can spread. Often, I feel like I should be doing something else–that I should not be going out to dinner, for instance, not because I do not want to, but because I do not think that I should be–I should be getting myself to some other place that I want, and am meant, to be.

Perhaps it is some form of guilt. I should not be playing because I should be working on getting to where I want to go, achieving what I want to achieve, fulfilling some purpose. Perhaps it is the thought that I will have to answer for not being in that place, not that anyone but myself necessarily has those expectations. The point is, if I am not getting to where I think I should be on some alleged higher path, I may as well be in the middle of the ocean, with no sense of how far I am from shore, too afraid to see if my feet can touch the bottom, and I envision the water being more than me, drowning me.

Imagine, I wake up in the ocean and I do not know how I came here. I have not opened my eyes yet, because I am afraid of what I might see–maybe the shore is nowhere to be seen. I am treading water but have not extended my toes to see how close the bottom of the ocean is. The shore could be swimmable. The depth may be shallow enough for me to reach easily. But I could also be in the middle of the sea with no land in sight, or perhaps worse, land I can see but too far away for me to swim to. The bottom of the ocean could be inches away, and I do not have to worry about having the energy to tread water or swim. Or not. I am certain that I cannot be here like this forever. Here is my anxiety. I do not know if I can make it out of the ocean, but I do know that I should not be where I am, and I cannot be here forever. The water will quietly swallow me, without even a gulp.

2.13: Where It Goes (Where Anxiety Takes Your Mind)

In something normal, something everyday, things start. Going to the grocery store, for instance. You need food for the week. You have done it a thousand times. It is a market that you have been to before and you know the routine and layout pretty well. But your mind does not walk you through the aisles normally. It does not follow the route from your house to the store, to the check-out and back home unloading your trunk.

Anxiety takes you to the next worst step. Not necessarily the worst case scenario, but bad enough, at least. You are hyperventilating in the store. You cannot breathe, and you are weak. You cannot make it back to your car, and even if you could, what would happen if somebody saw you, turning red, walking away from your cart, and now someone else had to take that cart and return everything to the shelves. You have made it their problem. Or you collapse, and someone has to find you. What will they think?

Your mind, with anxiety, does not bring you through what you know, or what you have experienced. It brings you through a negative play, that dredges up uneasy physical reactions sometimes, which in turn fulfill your fears, which bring up more physical reactions. It has gone to a place that is simultaneously familiar–you know what feels bad, and what panic attacks are like–but also unfamiliar, in that it is not based in a world that you are actually experiencing at that moment.

It has taken you totally within your mind, into a world that claws the physical along with it. it is so familiar, but not friendly.

2.14: Anxiety, Panic, and Depression

When our anxiety feels hopelessly permanent in the face of what we cannot deny, we become depressed. When our anxiety searches for an answer and is faced with an outcome that we will not accept, we panic.

Anxiety and depression are not separate modes. They are shades of the same personal incongruity with the world. We associate depression with sadness, and panic with frantic energy. When I am panicking, I am flailing. When I am depressed, I am resigned.

In both cases, I am uneasy with where I find myself. It does not feel right. When I feel there is no exit, I am depressed. When I want to tear through the room, I panic.

2.15: Natural State

I used to think that a person's natural state in the world could not be one of conflict. But what happens when the world itself is in conflict with you, and you are forced into it? It does not matter how reasonable or moral you are. If across from you is lunacy, you have no choice but to activate that fight or flight response. The issue is not you, though. It is them.

The philosopher Thomas Hobbes said that he was born with a twin: fear. According to a legend that Hobbes himself established, he was born prematurely when his mother had a panic attack when she heard the news of the Spanish armada sailing to England. Whether or not this is true, it is a reflection of an internal state that he felt was core to his being, and its relationship to the world. It shaped his thinking and philosophy.

We can reason all that we want. We can talk it out in our heads, or with that world across the table from us. But they are not hearing it. Thomas Paine, a revolutionary American thinker, said that arguing with someone that was unreasonable was like administering medicine to a dead man. We can ask ourselves if we are willing to treat our irrational adversary as a lost cause. Regardless, the argument playing out of our anxiety is killing us.

I know my mind. I know my desires. I know how I think it should be. But there are other ideas telling me: *no.* Limitations become corporeal. There is disagreement and it cannot be resolved amicably. I can change my behavior. Adjust. But even when I yield, it feels like there is always more to give. At a certain point, when I am my most exhausted, I have no more to give. It has become too heavy to lift the weight.

So I do not want to fight. I am a pacifist at heart. I am conflict averse. But you are forcing me into a fight. The weight of the world is heavy and it continues to pile on more. My strength has waned and my will has given in. It is becoming too heavy for me to lift.

2.16: Heights

Everyone is afraid of heights–just different heights.

I remember climbing the Tower of Mangia in Siena, in Italy. The buildings of the town are actually the rusty color sienna. The tower overlooks Piazza de Campo, the main plaza in the town. The edges of the area are lined by cafés and shops, with streets branching off into light brown mazes, with balconies on all sides of you, giving the impression that you are in a ceiling-less room, with people always ready to lean over and pluck you from the ground. The streets wind into other open spaces, smaller plazas, and sites to view hilltop vistas that remind you that you are in Tuscany, albeit in what seems like a brickwork single edifice making a multi-tiered town.

The tower itself is 367 feet (102 meters) tall. It is taller than the Statue of Liberty. The cathedral in the city is the same height, symbolically equal.

To get to the top of the medieval structure, you take the stairs. You walk straight up the brick and marble structure, with windows giving you an idea of your distance above street level, wide open to the air every so often. You come to a fairly open top and survey the land. Maybe at this point, your legs are shaky, fully seeing how far from the earth you are, but also how close you are to the edge, finding the railing with your hands.

An interesting thing happened on the way up. I was not afraid when I took the first step, or the second step, or even the third. Ten steps, twenty steps, thirty steps in, there was no fear. I do not know exactly how many stairs it was when it became too much. The stairwell of the tower, with its three foot thick walls and tight turns, obstructs your perception of height most of the way. At a certain point, though, it was too high for me.

I did not panic, but I did feel fear. I am too far up—the thought coursed through my body. My legs were weak. I did not want to approach the edge of the landing. I never considered myself afraid of heights, but here I was, afraid of being too high.

Every stressor affects us. Our ability to live with and process stressors is always changing. A stressor like a height my not require much in the way of emotional processing when it is a small height that we are accustomed to or comfortable with. Raise that height, and the mental requirement also grows, until there is a break and we are anxious. In a converse reality, a small stressor may not under most circumstances worry us. But during a particularly stressful time or on a bad day, that small stressor overwhelms us. It sets us off.

Stressors exist along with our capacity to manage them. An imbalance of either, whether in a single experience or perpetually, can make you anxious and possibly panic. Everyone is anxious, just at different levels, with different triggers. We all have different capacities.

2.17: Reminders

Everything is a reminder of what you cannot do because of anxiety.

I remember seeing a Congressional hearing on television. I do not know what it was for, but I remember it making me anxious, not because of the topic or the tension of the conversation, but because I immediately put myself in the imaginary position of having to speak in that room, and not being able to do so. I am afraid of the travel. I am afraid of the public display. I am afraid of being required to be available and attentive on a schedule that is not my own. What would I do if I was called? Would I ask for some type of accommodation? That would be embarrassing but maybe the best bet to quell the anxiety. Would I just not go and risk being sent to prison on charges of contempt? And what would happen if I went to jail? Unable to leave, away from the safety of my own home, how would I react? Would that reaction be a panic attack? What would happen if I had a panic attack in a cell? Better not get arrested.

These are ridiculous thoughts, of course. They are so far outside of the realm of what is likely that spending much mental energy on them is a waste. But it is effective on a person with chronic anxiety or depression. The lack of control. The helplessness. These themes can be found virtually anywhere, constantly reminding you that *you cannot handle it.*

That is what they all say anyways. Are those thoughts right? Are they self-fulfilling? Are the reminders anything more than the fear itself? It is all so pervasive that it is no wonder we often feel tired, constantly live anxiously, even when actually not living these scenarios.

2.18: On One Side Is the Mind and on the Other Is the World

On one side is the mind and on the other is the

world. The mind is constantly trying to make sense of the world. The world is constantly imposing itself.

When our minds are able to reach into the world and apply reason in vast ways, the mind can be at play, approaching the sublime. Think about when we watch a movie or hear music, and our minds wander over it, making connections that are not explicit, deciphering the lesson of the poetry. This is what it looks like when our imaginations take control.

But when the world dominates, stress and anxiety rise from the ground. The world is unreasonable. It is chaotic. It is like smoke—hard to define a shape, impossible to hold.

So when I ask, "Why do I have to defeat anxiety? Why do I have to figure it out?" The answer is: that is what we always do, because that is what we want to do. We try to figure everything out, as part of our nature. We apply reason to everything. We make a narrative. We create a world. We apply meaning. It feels good to do these things. We may be prompted, and led, and influenced in ways that we would object to if they were more obvious, but nonetheless it is a creation. It is our natural state. Why? Because we do.

2.19: Acting Out

We act out. Sometimes, it is in bad ways. Ways that hurt others. The irrational—or inability to have the rational—leads to our own irrational behavior.

I am anxious, uneasy, irritated, confused, unsure of

what to do, and wanting it all to make sense—to bend to my way. I can resolve this conflict in a number of different ways.

I can withdraw: totally not engage with the situation that is in front of me. This is maybe the least destructive way to negatively respond. Situations are all different, and the people around you may not appreciate it. But it is generally better than the below options.

I can be erratic: make my moves wildly, without reason or deliberate thought, oblivious to the consequences. Sure, sometimes just going with your gut and intuition is a good thing, but to what extent is even the unconscious guiding hand involved? No, it is having a logical progression and then jumping to an action irrelevant of the preceding.

I can be violent: the world does not fit my sense of it, so I must force it to comply, by any means necessary, disrespectful of all that surrounds me. Everything is scary, and I am anxious. That terror that I feel activates the fight or flight response, and when I fight, it is with anything in my vicinity. Blame is placed just because you are seen, not because it is thought rationally. I am afraid, feeling alone, in a world that I do not understand. It must be destroyed and remade to fit me.

I can be all around terrible: unpleasant. Negative to all and about everything. I do not enjoy what I am feeling, and as an extension nothing can be enjoyed. This is the most interesting as it is almost like a learned behavior. An internalization, in a different way, of the anxiety, to the point where it becomes external as we direct that energy back out to the world. The movement between realms. One feeding from the other, here in a negative way.

2.20: Pregnant Pause

Imagine a musical performance. Or a lecture. Or anything with a presenter and an audience. The show is about to begin and the performer is introduced by a voice offstage. The performer walks on to welcoming applause.

Typically, there is a quick "Thank you," or a timely launch into the first number. But what if instead there was silence. The applause dies down. The room becomes quiet. There is a pause. It is a time between the audience's reaction and the performer's opening. We might not realize it, but we are conditioned to a certain cadence. If it is broken at that meeting point, we notice.

Imagine you are in that audience. What are you thinking as you wait, as what you expected to be met with, is not met there? Do you feel excited? Is it a positive excitement or a negative excitement? What are you expecting now? Is it different than what you anticipated before that break in expectations? How difficult is it to describe your expectations at that point?

It is in this space, in this pregnant pause, that anxiety is born.

Chapter 3

3.1: Anxiety Is Not New

Anxiety is not a new phenomenon. Check the history of literature and philosophy. Go back as far as you want and I am sure that you can find it. Did you feel the nervous energy in the air in Plato's cave?

The fulcrum of anxiety in philosophy always existed with Kierkegaard, Sartre, and Camus (with non-philosopher-in-title-only Dostoevsky seated at the same table). We can talk about the Stoics, about Spinoza, about Merlou-Ponty, or just about anyone else if you like. If you look for it, you will always find it. But it is with the hands of the small cabal mentioned above that Continental and Existential class notes are written.

The reputation of Existential philosophy is well known. The focus on the darker aspects of our mental lives forces the reader to ask uncomfortable questions about themselves, their own existence, and their agency in life. Does the world have any meaning? Why bother trying to transcend anxiety? Why bother at all, right?

Although anxiety is not always in that most hopeless and resigned of realms, it is on the same continuum.

These are questions that truly we can only ask ourselves. Kierkegaard sees freedom as our point of anxiety. Sartre and Camus were surrounded by a world in the throes of war, full of consequential choices. Their work always has with it the specter of death. Camus is perhaps the most blunt, facing suicide head-on. With the situation that one finds themself, he asks: is life worth living?

What is absurd about my situation? I am comfortable in my office. I am fortunate to have all of my needs taken care of. I can say that I have more than I need to survive, in fact. But I cannot escape it: why bother? I feel this even when I am not in my most resigned and desperate state. Why go on with the world, and why go on with this feeling of anxiousness? This was the anxiety of those that came before us. It was inextricably intertwined as the effect of something else: Freedom. Absurdity. The conditions may have changed, but how our minds work has not.

And it is true: that open space of imagination and irrationality has always been anxiety inducing. There is a reason we sometimes call it nerves. It is in us, wrapped within the fibers of our bodies. The anxiety comes from us and always has.

3.2: The Anxiety of Their Times

All traditions have examined the anxiety of their

times. The hopelessness of each individual situation has been found and confronted. Anxiety itself is not unique to a time, the objects of anxiety just change.

When we think about anxiety in the philosophical context it is often anxiety about Big Things. Existential dread, angst, and restlessness are confrontations with a nervousness that is both inside (our own thoughts) and out (observed with others, socially and culturally at the time), and encompasses our being itself. We ask ourselves what it all means. Does it mean anything? We wonder how it could be "like this". What is this human condition that we find ourselves in?

The peak of the Existentialist tradition, overlapping with great phenomenologists, was at the same time as the atrocities that World War II brought in the first half of the twentieth century. The implications of modernity were also front and center for many, altering society for better or worse. With this, the individual experience of anxiety led to a turn and look outward, simultaneously something experienced on one's own, but used to search for sibling experiences.

This is the nature of the conversation, and the way that we inevitably talk about anxiety. We understand it most when it is our own, and when speaking about it, we extend it to the universal and generic. Traditions of anxiety did the same: they encountered anxiety and memorialized it.

3.3 Attempts to Find the Answer

Attempts to find the answer to anxiety are immeasurable. Do you think that anybody that has ever looked for it has actually found it?

Has anybody found how to defeat anxiety? Does anybody know why we should transcend anxiety?

Have we made progress toward the answer? Consider these regimens: The pills seem to help, but not cure, and in doing so create their own, new, chronic struggle. The therapies help us get through the day, but it is not quite enough. It is setting the bar either low, or someplace that is not exactly where we want to be now. The quote and axioms that people repeat and post over and over are not some kind of magic mental elixir either. How long has anyone lived according to a single saying? There is always another—another attempt to remind us about some kind of peace that maybe never existed.

There are always new versions as well. We change, tweak, and adjust. Sometimes we just start again from scratch. Despite it all, our anxiety, both collectively and individually, is chronic. It cannot be excised, it seems.

So is the answer knowable and we just have not found it? Have we resorted to "get through the day" therapies and medications and whatever else because that is the best that we can do? Have all the attempts failed? The attempts to describe anxiety seem to be descriptions of shadows. But maybe it is the personal nature of anxiety that is to account for this.

Structurally, anxiety seems to be described by academia and medicine through its effects–what it does to us. This is not without some merit, but it also hammers on that time honored tradition of treating the symptoms and not the causes.

We are not off the hook personally either. Our own attempts to describe anxiety are always being revisited. Our own attempts to get past anxiety are always exhumed. Our own attempts to find a reason are always evaluated, forgotten, remembered, and re-evaluated over and over again. Is it human nature to perpetually change? Or is that more of an indictment on the attempts and explanations themselves?

Maybe, looking for reasons is only part of it, and we should be looking for the modality that it lives in–that anxiety exists in. How does it come to be, not necessarily personally, although that is important, but as something that exists in our existence?

So, no, the answers have not been found despite centuries of questions. The attempts to find the what and the why have been cries for help. I empathize. I feel for them. I am them. I do not want to admit that anxiety is unknowable except through its symptoms. We are too intimate with anxiety for it to remain a stranger.

3.4: Anxiety Through Western Thought

At what point do we recognize the anxiety that has permeated through philosophy is not an aberration or a tangent, but it is a feature. It is not just part of a school of thought, a preoccupation, or an element of a specific time. It is intrinsic to thought. It is who we are.

The Existentialist tradition is the most obvious, and explicit, of anxiety laden philosophical thought, along with the adjacent literature and philosophy of the era. Camus is a standard bearer, and Kierkegaard is obviously a giant of dread as well. Sartre's *Nausea* is a clear signpost. Heideger's discussions of angst as one of our essential features elevated our nervousness as a mood, for certain. (When Heidegger talks about the readiness of things and finds that in their broken state he can fully understand what they are, is this not a point of anxiety, where things are not as they should be, and our attempt to put them back together?) This is just to name a few.

We can look further back, though. The struggle to overcome in Nietzsche is familiar to the anxious. Hegel's conflicted arguments are an uneasy clash of ideas—an incongruence. Hobbes felt fear in utero, so he says, with the Spanish Armada sitting just offshore. Augustine is on a search for peace in the world, as he searches for God and his way to live.

Even Plato's allegory of the cave, cut-off, trying to make sense of a universe out of reach through unfriendly shadows, is fraught with fear and trembling. It is a scary place that we are trying to make sense of.

For how long have we seen this in art as well? To name an extreme few, Pasternak's *Dr. Zhivago*, Ellison's *The Invisible Man*, and essentially all of Dostoevsky vibrate with anxiety.

What are the shared characteristics of all of these? Firstly, there is the separation between what is and what should be, with differing ideas about the origin of the "should". Throughout there are strong ideals and weighted opinions. Secondly, there is the identification that the burden of interpretation lies within the person, stated either explicitly or implicitly. Even when speaking about collectives, the individual is still the key component. Where there is divergence is on whether this understanding is achievable, and if it is, how one goes about it.

3.5: Hysteria

Anxiety was used as a diagnosis of weakness, and as such placed as a label on members of society that were seen as weaker. Until the beginning of the twentieth century, "hysteria" was used to describe an anxious, panicked state, but only when describing women. Even now, over a hundred years later, calling a woman "hysterical" can still be heard as a slur.

In the aftermath of the first World War, soldiers returning from the battlefield with "shell shock" expanded the understanding of who could be anxious, and hysteria was not solely an affliction of females.

In T. S. Eliot's 1915 poem, "Hysteria", this gender dynamic is displayed. Eliot's first wife had displayed signs of psychological distress, but it is unclear if it had fully manifested itself yet when he published the poem. It is written in long, prose-like sentences, emphasizing a frenzied situation that builds upon itself. The speaker's dinner companion hysterically laughs, disturbing other patrons we are led to infer, as a harried waiter urges them to relocate their dinner to the garden. The embarrassed speaker attempts to salvage the afternoon by somehow calming his companion.

Close to the surface, it is obviously the woman who is hysterical and anxious in an explicit sense. But in behavior, our analysis cannot limit the diagnosis there. The waiter, repeating his request for relocation, displays unease. The speaker, ashamed and set to change the reality that he finds himself in, is showing his own panic as well, even if he does not find himself to be similarly in distress.

Whether purposely or not, the poem is not only a study of a situation that depicted sexist tropes, but even more so a demonstration of anxiety's universality. That it was written just as a culture was learning of its myopic, wrongheaded view, makes it all the more intriguing. The woman's anxiety in the poem was intolerable to the other characters. But if they looked at their own unease, they would have found similarities, and how they shared in this human condition.

3.6: Anxiety Morphs Across Time

Is the anxiety of our forebearers the same as our anxiety?

I am not asking that question literally, of course. First of all, each of our anxieties is our own. Only I can experience my anxiety—I cannot make you experience it, just like you cannot give me yours. We can understand, though. Relate. Empathize. Our anxiety shares features, shares flavors, the colors and shades are the same. The object of our anxiety may be the same. The pressures and stressors can be shared, or seen the same by all of us. My anxiety can also transform into a pressure on you. But even still, the anxiety is each our own, with the weight of the outside world working in concert with our own, unique internal sculpting techniques to create something that will always be our own personal unease.

Secondly, on balance, the conditions are not the same. We are not living through the Russian Revolution in Saint Petersburg. We have our own battles—some literal and some not—but not less trying. However, this is not to say that the same threats—the world conditions that contribute to our anxieties—necessarily disappear. Nor does it mean that our predecessors' anxieties have no bearing on our own.

The threat of a nuclear war was a source of nervousness and existential crisis for many. As I write this now, nuclear weapon stockpiles have reportedly been cycled down, however still to levels that rival the decade or so immediately after Hiroshima and Nagasaki, when the collective fear of war juiced up by atomic weapons was at its highest. The number of actors with a nuclear arsenal has increased since them. So are we safer now than our grandparents and great-grandparents were? Is there reason to feel the fear that they felt? As a people, our attitude and attention to such a threat has waned. The stimuli have faded, at least for the time being.

This is not to say that a weakened shared anxiety does not have an effect from generation to generation. It is more the case that one anxiety does not beget an anxiety that is the same, or even looks the same. Take for instance a parent's fear of their child being abducted. The chances are slim, but during the 1970's and 80's, it was a pervasive anxiety amongst Americans. I am sure that this fear continues to be very real for some people. But imagine growing up with a parent that dealt with this anxiety daily, and in an effort to mitigate it, kept their child close. Never letting them stray too far. Always checking-in. Never alone. Constantly clear that the connection to one another and communication of whereabouts were paramount to daily life.

Now, consider that child growing up and having to be away from that parent, whether it be when they go to school, or leave the house, or when the parent has to go out without the son or daughter. That fear of abduction that the parent had may have spawned a fear of abandonment or separation anxiety in the child. One anxiety giving birth to another.

As we grow older and find ourselves in situations that we remember our parents being in, we also feel a pressure to be different: to not make the same mistakes, or transcend and be better than our parents were.

On a macro level, our collective attention shifts, from worry to worry, with new concerns taking the place of old, even while what we conceive of as threats may still remain. In our personal lives, the anxieties of those around us weigh on us in different ways, and often, can produce anxieties inside of us that are entirely different than that which we become a second level victim of.

The anxiety in the air is an anxiety that we breathe. But we process it differently. Call it differently. Anxiety does not spring from nothing, and sometimes it is from what comes before us.

3.7: Violence at the Beginning

Think of all the great anxious existential works that start with or center on an act of violence.

The violence comes in two ways: as an act that breaks the reality of the person seeing or experiencing it, or an act committed by a protagonist as a lashing out against the reality in which they find themself.

Hamlet's father is murdered, breaking the Prince

of Denmark's world, and he attempts to solve and ultimately right this wrong in *Hamlet*.

Raskolnikov heinously butchers two people, and struggles to reconcile that version of himself in the world with the extraordinary and noble man that he believes himself to be in *Crime and Punishment*.

Meursault kills the man on the beach, wrought with confusion in an indifferent world full of others with their own emotional expectations of him in *The Stranger*.

The violence does not have to be physical. It can all happen within one person's story. Sisyphus lived a life of awfulness towards others and was sentenced to a punishment of desperation. The titular character in *Invisible Man* trounces through the violence that surrounds his school, eventually being personally assaulted through banishment from it, only to find more violence in the north, forced eventually to try to break free via his own rebellion.

Through it all, the conflict between the person and the world dominates. The violence may be inflicted upon individuals, and it is no doubt painful to these characters, but as characters they are also monuments to more than a single person. A being themself is in conflict with this world around them, we are shown. They are both broken from the normal flow of the world, and attempting to break from the flow that they find themselves in. It is a broken relationship.

How does repair come? Often it is through the most extreme of escapes in these stories. Too often, it is not what we would call a happy ending. But is that the characters' fault? Or is it that they are always bound to lose, up against an adversary that is not even playing the game. The world is not trying to be in conflict. It simply is a conflict to the individual. Get with it, or get out.

These are stories. They are contained between hardcovers. They are meant to tell us something. The conflict is between them and the world that they find themselves in. There is a disagreement. Something does not match. So, they rebel. They laugh in its face. There is a tear in their eye. And there is a plot.

In our minds, we are trying to construct a plot. But how many more pages do we have left to go?

3.8: How Come So Much is Written about Anxiety in Times of Upheaval?

How come so much is written about personal anxiety during times of upheaval? How come we read so many explorations of one's own angst that are set against times of change?

Meanwhile these protagonists, both real and imagined, phase in and out of the cause, unsure. They feel the larger battle is not in the streets, but in their own heads. The internal unease finds parallels to the external world. Comrades in arms appear. The personal stresses become shared stresses. That something is not right, is reinforced.

Surely now, when the world is on fire, everyone

will understand how in fact here, in my chest, there is also a fire.

But when is the world ever not on fire? And when is it never not burning inside of me?

3.9: Why Does Anxiety Keep Coming Up?

No philosophy, no tradition, no method, no therapy, and no pill has rid us of anxiety. You would be hard pressed to find someone that has struggled with anxiety and depression to honestly say that they are totally free and clear of it, even if they have worked to reduce its effects in their lives to as low as they can push it.

Anxiety survives. Panic is always a possibility. The traditions persist, and the questions keep getting asked. New approaches are made and new perspectives are had.

It could be viewed as a function of the world constantly changing, and throwing new stresses at us, forcing us to react, and that newness takes time for us to adjust to, to wrap our minds around, and to make part of our reasoning. But in that perspective, it makes us sound like we are unfit for the world. We are the ones that are incongruent with the universe's constant state of change, it says.

But I am of the world. I am not a piece that does not belong. It is out of habit that I adjust. I do not owe the world my adjustment.

So why does anxiety keep coming up? It comes up

as I try to make sense of a thoughtless, inconsiderate world—a world that cares nothing for me. In my fight against that, the struggle is my anxiety. Absorbing the blows, while not physical, requires my mental and emotional reaction. It keeps coming up because the world is relentless.

But so is my mind. My mind will not stop reasoning. This conflict, this place of collision, is the natural state of things.

3.10: Blow Up the Outside World

The general approach and treatment for anxiety disorders has been focused on the individual and their internal factors. There are some fair reasons for this. It is only one's self in their own mind. It is the individual that enters treatment. A situation or a society cannot enter therapy. You cannot prescribe a pill to heights, or spiders, or airplanes. Or the open world outside of your house. Or your family situation. Or lack of opportunity and success. Or death. It is easier to work with the individual and to change the way that they are situated to the world affecting them and its effects.

But is it better? Is it actually addressing causes or effects?

Take for example a person that is anxious because their life is unfulfilling. The promise of their youth has disappeared as they enter another period of their life. They enter a regime meant to assuage them with what they have, and to accept the things that they cannot change. To an extent, that is necessary. They need their job in order to make a living in order to pay for what they need to survive. Perhaps this is not just for themself, but also for a family that they are to support. What does accepting these things do for one's nervousness, though?

Changing your attitude towards your surroundings, while necessary in some cases, leaves intact the conflict that led to the angst. It is not a contest, but it does let the world win. Your mind and your feelings have subjugated themselves to the external factors that have borne down against you. Indeed, you have given a part of yourself up. Without changing the world around you, it will always have the upper hand, and increased strain, and perhaps a relapse to a worse depression will loom.

Consider the uneasy person who is described as always searching. If they give up the search, they end unfulfilled. The incongruity remains. Whether they know what they are searching for or not, they know that something is missing. It does not have to be found at the expense of what they have. And the treasure does not have to necessarily be exactly what they think that they are looking for or need. But it has to be something.

Rather than the person always changing—and the change will be recurring, as a person continually has to adjust to the stressors of the world as it is—the world can change also. The aggressor is the world. The traditions that have probed anxiety have always seen this conflict. The situation does not make sense, so bending the world to make it make sense, needs to be an option.

The world refuses to recognize us. Let us make it.

Chapter 4

4.1: Who Will Survive? Who Wants to Live?

Who will survive? Who wants to live? When there is anxiety in every second that we live?

We are born innocent. We build a worldview. The world is not easy. Turn on the news: Disease. Natural disasters. Evil men out to get you. But you can leave the dramatics aside and still see it. Every day, waking up, going to a job you do not want to do. You would rather stay in bed a little longer. Spend time with your family and friends. Have something a little better to eat or drink. Go to sleep a little later than you should, as if you will not pay a price because nothing is forcing you to wake up early. But that is not the world that you live in. The world is insisting there be something else. The world is putting more on you.

There is always some kind of demand that cuts into the day that you want, the day that you think that you should have.

But things seem to be getting worse, right? (It is irrelevant if they actually are or not. It is what it *seems*.)

More famine. More storms. The Earth is warming. Bad men are doing things in your name. It is harder to get what you want. A feeling of security is harder than ever to come by. Stability, if you ever believed in it, is more difficult than ever to hold on to.

Will you be able to hold on to it? For your family? For yourself? You are told that what you think you should have is not what you will have. That you have to work harder to get less. The cost of living is going up. Food is becoming more scarce. Plagues are among us.

Did you need all of this? Did you not have enough to worry about already? A walk down your street can be filled with tension. Will you make it through?

And if you do, for what? You have just tortured yourself. Tired yourself out during daylight hours. There is no energy left for yourself. You have survived, but at what cost? And now you have got to do this again tomorrow?

Something has to give. Something has got to change.

4.2: In the Air

Collective spikes of anxiety across time have something in common: they come at times when there is great social upheaval. The world that people knew is fading, and a new one is emerging. There is change, and they try to catch-up with it. Indeed, the World Wars and the march of modernity provided a fertile context for existential thinkers. Political upheaval created dissidents, soldiers, and psychologists, all attempting to make sense of what they were experiencing.

In *Dr. Zhivago* there is a line that states it plainly: "We are faced with the rise and spread of a form of psychic illness that is typical of our time and is directly related to the contemporary upheavals." If mass anxiety is a thing, if it is possible, it is because of something outside of each of us. A shared experience must be contributing to the nervousness.

When we talk about anxiety, we focus on our internal dialogue, and make the external secondary. We focus on our interpretation of events, and often demote the events themselves. In post-traumatic situations, this makes some sense, as the past cannot be changed, even though structures that buttress that moment in time can be assessed. But it is that externality that presents itself that is at issue here. Our minds had been prepped and were cruising along. When considering the atrocities of war, should we look at the patient and say, "well, you have just got to find a way to adapt to it, to change your thinking."

How callous is that? To tell the person hurting that it is they that have to change their ways–that it is them that is out of sync with the rest of the world. While it may be true in fact that the rhythms do not match, it puts the fault and responsibility on that individual. On us.

These shared events, cultural changes, shifts in society, something in the air–all affect us, and sometimes they change us in profound ways that are obvious, and sometimes not so obvious. And sometimes, they are difficult for our minds to assimilate with. It can easily cause a break. It leads to what we experience as anxiety. It is yet another launching point for us to feel panicked and crushed.

4.3: Social Anxiety

It seems more common to hear that someone experiences social anxiety than that someone enjoys company. That does not necessarily mean that more people are socially anxious than are not, or that they are all actually socially anxious, but it does reflect some possible truisms.

First, we are all under social and societal pressures. The rise of social media and the culture around it breeds a state of constant comparisons and contrasts between each of us. It places a premium on sharing, particularly on sharing something that will garner different forms of clout. Desires to fit in or being accepted existed before, but the addictive nature of online ecosystems make it all the more prevalent in our lives. Furthermore, it offers clear, quantified measures of vindication or negation. Now the stories that we told ourselves about whether or not we are accepted or not are backed up by data. Of course, the data is arbitrary and stilted, and we choose to fit it to the narrative however we choose. Nonetheless, it furthers interpersonal anxieties that already exist, and prioritizes homogeneousness in how we relate (or not relate) to others, with a primacy over an appearance of authenticity, often at the expense of authenticity itself. There is an irony to authenticity being valued in what people consume, but less so in what they deliver, beyond its appearance.

Second, it is an indicator of something never said: we are all anxious. Does anyone actually think that they are "normal"? Does anyone not have what we would call quirks? Does anybody have zero secrets that they keep to themself, sharing only perhaps with their most personal of relations? And what is the driving factor of these non-traditional, socially acceptable behaviors and thoughts? In many cases, it is the result of a conflict between what the world expects of us and what we believe or want. We compensate for that discordance and the feeling that something is not right.

Indeed, most anxiety can perhaps be called social anxiety if we look at it a certain way. We are in a constant state of angst when faced with that world around us.

4.4: The Cup of Modernity

How many decisions are made with an eye towards what makes life worthwhile?

How many decisions that we make for others, or that are made for us, are with an eye towards what is worthwhile in life?

Yet they are all made. The decisions have been made

over time, snowballing, gathering mass, continuing to roll towards us, over us, and eventually past us.

Modernity has always been a race to the west. A competition to see who could get furthest towards the end. Take a break and breathe and you know–there is no end. The world is round and it will keep going.

Yes, as modern life continues to push and push towards some goal, pushing us as a means towards that goal. We envision success. For each of us, success looks different: maybe it is peace. Maybe it is rest. Maybe it is riches. Maybe it is stature. Maybe it is any number of things that live within your heart. But modern life does not tell us that there is anything that is enough. It is always asking for more, asking to keep going further. More, bigger, faster, stronger.

Modernity gives us things to aspire to, but never lets us achieve them. We think we should, but the world does not deliver. The forever grasping, the exhaustion, the incomprehensibility of indifference, the conflict of beliefs, is enough to put you on edge. It is a stressor, lurking. It pushes us. If it does not make us anxious itself, it points us in that direction. It fills the cup enough, so that it takes less to overflow it.

4.5: Pandemic

This book was conceived, and writing started, before a once-in-a-century global pandemic began in 2019.

Millions of people–maybe even billions–suddenly saw the world that they knew change. It is forever changed for some of us. What they knew and expected no longer was. People reacted in different ways. Some were able to adjust with some angst, but ultimately transitioned to a different day-to-day way of being. Others rebelled in unhealthy ways. Some fought against ordinances that local authorities put in place for the benefit of the overall public. Their manifestations of anxiety did not look like the melancholy that is traditionally associated with anxiety and depression, but make no mistake, it is the same.

Perhaps it is all always the same when people act out, oftentimes violently. But because each person's anxiety is their own and we cannot fully experience and maybe even express it adequately between us, we just can never confirm it. The world that people knew was no more. Suddenly there were limitations. What they wanted to happen–and needed to happen–would not. Many felt that their freedoms were being infringed , and this loss could only be reasoned as an affront to their lives that they had to rage against. A virus that they cannot control does not fit into a worldview that demands the ability to do as they please.

But the virus, like the world, does not care. It is this awesome part of nature that can easily press down upon us indifferently. When it is a gorgeous horizon, we can feel sublime. When it is an invisible death, we can feel our smallness. Our minds reach for the capacity for each.

4.6: Baldwin

There is anxiety when someone finds that the world around them is one way, and they themself are not a part of it. This discovery is accompanied by a declaration of otherness. Of exclusion. It is imposing anxiousness. There is no rest and no peace when you are told that you are not welcomed to what is allegedly shared. The writer James Baldwin described this when explaining the awakening a young African-American child has when the vision of a just society is shattered by an unavoidable racism for the first time.

It is an experience that happens every day. It is a conflict that does not resolve itself.

How sensitive are we to these injustices? Beyond just the indignities we see, the material and the physical, the inconvenience and the exclusion, do we also feel for the beating of the minds? There are stressors that we can all relate to and there are stressors that we know in another, sometimes lesser, way. The struggle to survive is something that we all experience in some way. But that weight in our bag, carried through the city streets in one hundred degree heat, is heavier when it is weighed down by racial injustice, perpetuated on multiple levels. If a person's words can feel like a push into an anxious state, the constant pressure of a system requires an enormous amount of energy in return just to exist as oneself.

This is not to give some type of false equivalency. It is not saying, "We have more in common than we thought, and it is in our anxiety." No, it is to say that anxieties fray nerves in different ways, and for some of us, in ways in others that we ourselves will never fully understand. Simultaneously, we must also realize that we may be a part of that pressure that causes anxiety in others.

4.7: Social Anxiety, Again

A social anxiety exists—and I am not talking about "social anxiety" as a diagnosis.

Rather, there is an anxiety that exists in our society: one that travels socially, and is also communicated socially. Our society gives us an anxiety. Anxieties of The Bomb are not prevalent for most of us today. But an anxiety of climate fear that did not exist before, does for many today. The anxiety experienced by Depression-era Americans is gone. But displacement fears take hold amongst many in developing nations. What is around us travels through us, into us, collectively to a society.

It happens through direct experience, like if a natural disaster drives someone from their home, or through a communication, like if someone is told that their current way of living is in jeopardy. These are overlapping categories, as both are experienced by a person, however one is a direct experience and the other is a suggested experience or a warning of sorts.

Traumas that we directly experience are easy to explain as drivers of our anxiety. If my house was destroyed by a tornado, we can all understand why I would have a fear of tornadoes, and become anxious whenever a storm passes through. If I have a negative experience at a theater, it is understandable how that will taint my thinking whenever going to a show is mentioned or thought about.

However, we all have felt some anxiety or depression for either unknown reasons, or in reaction to the thought of something that we have not actually experienced, whether probable or not. We receive stimulants constantly. Information is sent, we receive, and it becomes something in our minds. Some of what we observe are stressors. A car barreling at us will cause stress. Cars are not supposed to come straight at us, and we have a reaction to that. Not everything is as obvious as a vehicle pointed at us to run us down.

Some of what we observe we interpret into a stressor. This may be the result of a trauma informing us. It may be the result of numerous experiences that add up to what our minds make into a negative situation. Sometimes, messages are made specifically to be stressors, even if they are not necessarily. We are influenced by stories that we hear, the framing of things, modeled behavior patterns, and out-and-out peer pressure. Yes, this sounds like "social anxiety", but recognize it is the social imparting the anxiety (or at least starting it), rather than your own anxiety about being social. Your fears are not unfounded. They came from some place, not out of thin air.

We recognize that something around us is not right.

We recognize that we are exhausted keeping up with the constant pressure placed upon us. We recognize that we are also not alone, even if it feels that way. Society simultaneously gives us things to be anxious and depressed about, all while demanding that we take part in that stressful society. It is a society that has anxiety pulsing through it.

4.8: Others

There is a line in Ralph Ellison's *The Invisible Man* that has given me some perspective on our own behavior in the society, culture, communities, and world that we live in. It says, "And sometimes the difference between individual and organized indignation is the difference between criminal and political action."

Our anxiety, isolated, can feel like a crime that we are guilty of. The unease or inability to face something, or to do something, feels like a betrayal on our part to everything and everyone around us. We apologize when we cannot get out of bed. We are sorry that we cannot make the party. You will think less of me if I am not able to ride that roller coaster with you. I am sorry to disappoint you, with my obvious failings of everything else that everyone else in the world is able to do. I apologize for not being "normal".

But if experiences and behaviors are shared things—as comrades in anxiety we are without fault. We are no longer less than what is demanded of us, what is required of us, in our lives. Suddenly marching to the beat of our own drum—which is difficult in our modern life—is not the sound of one drum, but of many. Even if it is not to the primary beat. Of course, this does not quell all anxieties (it may even exasperate some if fading into obscurity is a source of angst), however in a social sense, it may soften the look of the other at least.

4.9: Slipping

The tightrope that we walk everyday is raised, and the effort that is required for us to stay balanced increases with it. Whether that is the reality or not, in certain ways, our perception of the world makes it real in our minds. If we believe in a negative outcome, we act accordingly, and whether or not the bad comes to pass, we have already fallen. And the ground below is unforgiving.

At least we assume that. We may have never fallen to the ground, and never felt the collision. But experience tells us what the impact will be, and we believe it. At a certain height, not only do we fear hitting the ground, but we also fear falling, and that it may be inevitable. If you slip, gravity will grab you.

Our tightropes are our sidewalks and our hallways. They are in our homes and our offices. They are where we live. And it can feel like any slip will be more than a small trip. It will cause a chain reaction that will bring the whole thing down. We are afraid that with one slip, we will fall out of line with everything around us. Everything around us is unforgiving.

True or not, this is how it feels. This is how we are pushed. This is what the world around us and the times we live in put us all through. It is more than just trying to keep up–it is trying to survive. It takes perfect balance in order to partake in the world around us, with our friends, our families. In our neighborhoods, and in our social circles. In the workforce and at the restaurants. We have to go there, and any indication that we cannot or will not be there is a sign of weakness that will be taken advantage of. That getting weak in the knees is all that it will take to slip. And fall. All the way down. To the ground.

4.10: Harder, Better, Faster, Stronger

Harder, better, faster, stronger. It is what the world around us pushes us towards. Always actualizing, but never actualized. Becoming but never became.

If we work harder things will be better. Hard work, after all, is what we are supposed to do. But I am just wearing myself out. My ability to balance stress is failing. I feel weak. "Well you just have to lean in and good things will come if you work harder." This is not true. It is just habituating you to the rat race. And you are maybe too tired to care, if you are lucky.

There is always something better. There is always more out there. Because what you have is not good enough. You have to go get bigger. Get better. You are not good enough. Enjoying what you have, where you are, is not part of the equation. Always striving. Always out of reach. Always improving. You are never good enough. Do not ask me why. I like it here.

Everything all of the time. Get there now, because there is somebody that will get there in front of you, and if you do not do it now you will miss out, someone younger and prettier will take your place, as you are really already too old and past your prime, besides you missed your chance anyways because you were not fast enough, you did not capitalize, and now you are on the treadmill, just trying to survive, with all of those responsibilities you have to honor.

It is tough out there you know, and you have got to be strong. You cannot be weak. Show strength, always. Nobody has time for your crying. Nobody has time for you to feel weak. You have got to be able to handle it, for everybody else. As soon as you let your guard down, it will get you, trust me. No matter how smart you think you are, it is irrelevant. Your mind, your intelligence, is totally independent of your natural workhorse of a brain, constantly working, outworking, the rest of you, to find the right path to making sense of the world. But it does not always make sense. Do you see that? And what can you do about it? It is too much, and eventually it gets too heavy to lift. The weight has not even changed, you are just weaker. Worn down. Take a break. But that is when it really starts to get in your head. When you let your guard down. When you have a moment to rest.

All the bad thoughts roll in. Now you are not on autopilot, and as you start to process everything, it is all too much. Trouble falling asleep at night, because all of that anxiety that is in you is now able to be heard. Your mind is racing. It is faster. It is better at pushing you than your conscious thinking. Who did this to you? You did it to yourself.

Make it stop, you say. Make what stop? Nothing is doing anything. You cannot point to anything. Why are you putting so much pressure on yourself? I did not know that I was. What else do you not know? I thought you were smart. I thought you had control over your thoughts. They are your thoughts, after all. Right there in your own mind.

4.11: An Age

"The Age of Anxiety" adequately described a post-World War world in Auden's epic poem. The psychologist Rollo May dove deeper, seeing a covert age of anxiety and an overt age of anxiety. What would we call our time? Anxiety has not abated, even if the subject has changed. Concurrently, it has expanded within the lexicon. "Shell shock" and "hysteria" have given way to post-traumatic stress disorders and post-partum depression. That is not to say that no stigmas are attached, to say nothing of the cases where it is the stigma that feeds some of the anxiety. Rather, anxiety is prevalent in our lives, so much so that it risks being performative. But we know better. We know what it is to suffer these nerves.

Our age is one where anxiety exists, and anxiety can be beaten, they say. Take these pills. Talk to this councilor. Then get back out there and see you in a month. For how many months? Well, it takes some time for these first prescriptions and these first sessions to really do anything, and that is if you get the right combination, the right dosages. So it is going to take some time. But then, eventually, until when? Well, if you are lucky, one day just never again. If you are not, well, we are not sure yet. Probably forever. I mean, that is the way we all act. As if it is going to be forever. You will need something to take that edge off into your old-age.

It is the kind of thing that bred alcoholics. It still leads to addiction today. We have just traded it all off. Yes, the previous ages have never faded. The subject may have changed, but the object has not. The predicate stays the same. You are anxious. You are nervous. You are depressed. You are suicidal. You want it to stop.

But it does not stop. Ages go from one to the next. There is no break. There is no hard line drawn. Gradually things look different, but they never just vanish. The world keeps turning. The universe keeps expanding.

4.12: Hope

"Hope" is a popular construct in the current zeitgeist monoculture. It is hard for me to pinpoint exactly what the popular idea of "hope" is, though. Is it just a word, and everyone can interpret it how they want, with truly little perspective underneath the authors we hear? I guess it is something about, no matter how terrible things are, they can get better–you can get to some goal that is better than the present.

Consider what this is saying: it is an admission of how bad things are, or at least of how unhappy we are. Little examination generally of *why*, just that it is not good. We are under attack. It looks and feels hopeless. The heroes take away that hopelessness, apparently. They do not promise success. Just give hope. Generally the heroes always win anyways, so I am not sure how much hope actually mattered in the predetermined scheme of things.

It is hard for me to say how much hope as an idea has ever really mattered to me. Maybe I am just that negative and pessimistic. I do not think I am a pessimist. More of a skeptic, really. I do not think that things will turn out badly necessarily. But I do not think that they have to turn out well either. Who is to say? There are not any rules here. Life is not carefully plotted. It is not plotted at all. There is no arc to this story. If there is an arc, it is actually hard to say that it is written in a way that we would want, anyways. Today, we are more worried and anxious because things seem to be getting worse in a multitude of ways. This is all from my perspective, of course, but I do not think I would be alone in saying this. On balance, do you think that people are happier now than they were 20 years ago?

This is not to say that things are the worst that they have ever been. Clearly, in many ways, particularly material ones, human life has never been richer. That can be true, but emotionally, the opposite may be the case.

Personally, I find lost causes in the world to be more motivating. Rebellion and revolution, being counter-culture has an allure. Maybe it is my age. Maybe it is a relic of the anti-consumerist, contra-sell-out time that I grew up in. A defiant attitude, a creationist attitude of lost cause, can be just as powerful and with agency. Because that is how powerful the opposite of hope can be. Hopelessness is devastating when you feel that way about yourself. There is no reasonable escape. It is the bottom. That is just the way that I feel. So leaning into it, in a way, and going off of a non-rational belief to fight the rational position of hopelessness, is more helpful to me.

When I was particularly down once, my physician said something to me that was more helpful than anything one of my (very capable and helpful) mental health professionals had ever said. It was: "You don't have to feel this way forever." There was not any explanation with it. No reason for that. It was just a statement, totally against everything else that I was thinking. I suppose that gave me hope. But it was not a hope *in* anything. It was just a declarative opposing statement to the way that I was living and thinking. It had no basis in experience. But it gave me the will for something different in this world, regardless of whether it was true or not.

Chapter 5

5.1: Worth, Matter, Meaning

If the universe had no meaning, how would that make you feel? I am not talking about the feeling that we are helpless, that nothing that we do matters. I am talking about the significance of any thing out in the world, independently. To the universe, the single grain of sand on the beach is no more or less important than the diamond ring on your finger. For me, it is not the meaninglessness of the world itself that gives me anxiety. Rather, *my* meaninglessness is the source of my anxiety. The indifference of the world *to me* is what makes me uneasy, even as I type this. Do I matter? Does what I think matter?

This lack of worth is depressing. It is self-worth defining. The universe does not apply worth to anything. So where does it come from?

Ourselves. That is why we are so worried about what other people think. That is why we feel the pressures of society. It is because those outside forces can impose their priorities easily, drowning out our own voice in our head assigning worth. There are more of them than there are us, after all.

Realizing that these are man-made constructs (which are susceptible to nefarious intentions) affects the worth and the meaning that I apply to them. Who are they to say? What makes them right? This is not to say that they are always wrong so we should always be a counter-culture crusader. They are all worth questioning, though. It is worth prioritizing the examination of the pressures and the meanings that the world around us applies.

It is taken for granted how much these outside factors contribute to anxiety at this point. We say it, but it is so cliché we do not even think about it. Society tells us what we should be doing. It sets expectations. We internalize these expectations and feel them. Our minds have trouble integrating these expectations with what we want, or the way that we think that things should be. Oftentimes it is a jumbled mess, and we really do not even know what we want. Our thinking is an amalgamation of observations of causes and effects of the world, our own experiences, our own desires, and the perceived desires of the world, both natural and unnatural, around us. We are concerned with what others think because we are told to be concerned with what others think. We give meaning–often outsized meaning–to how we fit in. We accept the way that they tell us we should live.

In some ways, this is a good thing. Tools for survival have been passed down for generations. But that is at the most macro of levels. On a more personal level, the results are much more mixed. Somewhere in between, we have to be choosy. Who can we depend on to give us meaning? Where should we derive our worth?

Now I ask: What is more anxiety inducing? Nothingness, or emptiness? A universe with no meaning, or one with made-up, artificial meanings?

5.2: Is There an Ethical Reaction to Anxiety?

Is there an ethical reaction to anxiety? Is there an imperative to react to anxiety, whether it be our own, or that of others, both individually and more generally?

On their own, anxiety and depression, along with any other mental stress that you may want to include, do not in themselves demand a reaction, let alone one that is ethical or moral. The idea that if you are anxious you should do *x* or if you are depressed you should do *y* is without any metaphysical standing on its own–unless we want to propose that the metaphysical world itself contains an anxiety, that is, an incongruence that clashes with the order around it. It is not that far-fetched, if you believe in a metaphysics and the tension produced in the troubled agreements (or disagreements) of principles that constitutes an existential unease. Is this what Camus finds absurd? Is this Hegel's project in dialectics?

But that is a consequence of our thinking-through. It is the result of us, human beings, and our brains, being inserted into the world, and not being able to help ourselves. It is our demand for sense, because there is no sense, and no meaning. Our demand for meaning. Our requirement for a unified theory of what we see. We cannot help ourselves. My anxiety becomes the universe's anxiety.

Any call to act on anxiety is a second step. It is not a call from anxiety in itself, but a call that we make in response to something that cannot hear us. It is a call that we make under the influence of the world around us, but not the world underneath that world (or above, depending on your preferred perspective). If I am anxious, I do not have an obligation to respond to that stress, good or bad, in any way. Those rules are not there. If you are anxious, I do not have a duty to respond from the pure fact of the stress itself. Rather, our response loop is more likely due to the consequences of that anxiety, or from a morality anchored to attitudes of humanity. The universe provides no guidance.

Would you say that you are morally bound to clarify to the confused? Is there an ethics for the sad, who you comfort? There is no imperative to calm the scared. However, we categorize much of this, especially if it lasts for a time, as suffering. If you ask anyone on the street, you are more likely than not to hear that we should do what we can not just to ease people's suffering, but also do our best to prevent it. Would they say that we should ease people's anxiety? I think that most probably would say that yes, we should, as people living in a world with other people, try to make people less stressed. But they probably would not go so far as to say that it is an obligation. Would they say that we should prevent people's anxiety? That I am not so sure of. In today's world, there are real currents of resistance to making other people comfortable explicitly. One's own comfort trumps that of others.

It is interesting to think about how two people's comforts can clash. If your friend invites you to dinner at a crowded restaurant, it is likely not done as a challenge to your nerves, but it may have that unintended effect. Every invitation one person extends to another can expose an incompatibility. One person's sensibilities get to sit in a chair, while the other's are forced to stand, on hot coals, with no shoes on. In the realm of ideas, of feelings, and of reason, there is little to no room for compromise, it seems. But this is not a maxim. The behavior is a choice. Indeed, we choose to address anxiety, both our own and that of someone else. This can sound admirable when considering individual relationships and the way that we personally act to each other. But if we expand the scope and the focus becomes less defined, with personal connection lacking, the strength to prioritize another's anxieties weakens. The instinct to be brave for your child exists in a way that bravery for the common good does not. In fact, oftentimes society tells us that we should focus on suppressing our own anxieties for that of the nameless whole. Why would we choose not to reduce or play to the anxieties of the most people possible, though?

The answer should be obvious: because it makes us, ourselves, anxious. It cedes control. It supplicates our own reasoning for that of another. It says that easing the anxiety of others is more important than your own. This may be easier for some and more difficult for others. If you are chronically anxious, barely anything can sound more terrifying.

5.3: Then You Are Diagnosed

Then you are diagnosed.

Labels are placed on you. Definitions. Expectations. Anti-expectations. You are searching for sense around the nonsensical, and they give it to you–you have a disorder. An entry in a book, already written. An example. And you are placed within a lane. It leads down a road that others have traveled before with the same stops along the way. The same treatments. The same answers. Your mileage may vary, but the differences are minimal. It is not made for you. It is not unique.

Your anxiety is reduced to a specific affliction, like a virus that can be isolated and examined. Deconstructed and immunized. Replicated.

All of the build-up, with the twists and turns that you cannot exactly remember but your mind naturally navigated during your last breakdown is now resolved into a roadmap of a land you do not totally recognize.

Sure you can make out the landscape, but you know that it is not your land. It is not where you live.

Your anxiety is yours. Your diagnosis is not. It is useful for the industry trying to help you, but it is also incredibly demoralizing and depressing in its own right. It tells you that you are not special. You have lost yourself and the answer is not your own.

5.4: Stigma

To what extent is our anxiety and depression the effect of the social stigma of a behavior?

Take for example someone that is agoraphobic. They have a fear of leaving the house. Put aside why that fear exists for a moment. From that fear, there is an anxiety. They believe that they should be leaving the house. Going outside is, after all, what a normal person does, they think. The fear and the cultural conditions have produced a separate reaction, beyond just the fear of the outside world.

Imagine as another example someone that feels anxiety at the prospect of embarrassing themself in public. Without any material consequences, the nervousness exists only because they are worried that they will not fulfill a societal norm that they believe is expected of them. Beyond just this social anxiety, other anxieties act similarly. While practical reasons may be a part of the feelings of anxiety and depression one experiences when considering a situation, there also exists a part that is solely based on the fulfillment of what *should* happen in that situation as well.

My anxiety is not just that I will be sick, that I will be destitute, that I will be punished. It is also that I will be insufficient, or incomplete, in what I am supposed to be. The fullness that is expected of me, that I expect, will not come to be. It is the existential crisis, that is not of literal existence. The fear is not of dying, it is of living as broken.

In actuality, it is a worldview that is fraudulent, in a culture that is broken. Living up to the standards set arbitrarily does not matter. Unfortunately, we think it does.

5.5: Methods

Therapy attempts to get you back to normal. Medication attempts to make it bearable. All in the service of getting you back into the flow of a world which makes no sense: the world which does not work for you (but you must work for).

Our most common methods of treatment for anxiety today are focused on managing, not curing. Is there a cure? I do not know, but certainly the attempt to find it, to squash anxiety, is barely existent. Therapies today focus on changing your ways of thinking through minimizing the anxiety that you feel, so that you can continue on while experiencing it. It is about visualizing what will happen if your worst fears do happen–not what life is like without that anxiousness, and certainly not focused on eliminating the causes of that anxiety. Medication, meanwhile, is there to numb the feelings, to slow you down. Both paths, especially the therapeutic, focus on the symptoms.

The physical and practical are primary, they would have us believe. And why not? They are the easiest to spot, and the clearest to explain. They also explicitly connect each of us with the world. It is the science-ification of our minds. (In many ways, this is what psychology is to philosophy, and what some sects of philosophical thinking attempt to do themselves.) I cannot deny that some people do find success in this. But to what end? What is their purpose?

These methods seek to change our behavior, as if it is the behavior that must change. It takes as a fact that anxiety is a physical problem—an imbalance of chemicals, or a problem in practicality.

I am not going to tell you that these methods do not have their place. Immediate intervention is absolutely necessary for some of us at some times. Something to take the edge off to help us survive can also be helpful. But to me, it must be in the service of getting to the next level of improving the situation. How? It must be in us to change things, and part of that is identifying what needs to change. The priorities on changing the self, which prioritizes the world as it is that we find ourselves in, is without a base, though. Why it gets to win is without a foundation. Continuing the race for the prize, it is right to question why we are running it, and if the prize is worth it. The reinforcement of it all by therapies and pharmaceuticals is ok to cast doubt on.

But you must get back into it! they say. You must not miss work! You must go to this function! You must do it this way! If all of this means nothing to me, why do I have to engage with it? And why does it mean something to you, and not me?

5.6: Getting By

Unfortunately for many of us, it appears that we need something just to get by. Just to be right.

There is no triumph in just getting by. There is no celebration for making it through the day tortured. Yes, you made it to work. You counted the hours and hyperventilated in a bathroom stall. Sure, you can take a little pride in it. But that is no way to live. Desensitization to the situation is a transformation of the self. Ask yourself: what are you transforming into? Just being able to tolerate the world makes us sullen and callous. Floating above it all is not easy.

The world always lures us back, and for good reason. We have mouths to feed. Bills to pay. Getting back into the day is not just about being a cog in an abstract machine. The society that we take part in allows us to live, and helps us survive. The luxury of stepping away, and of resetting, is only available for the fortunate among us. That is not to say it is impossible.

But where would someone go? Often, that somewhere is counter to the culture. If I do not like being social, obviously being antisocial is the escape route. But who wants to be anti- anything? It is set up and framed as a negative. Now, I can try to work around the social aspects of life, if I choose. But it would take work, and the world has a way of trying to pull you back into it.

Imagine it is not just about being social. Imagine your anxiety is riding on public transportation. You hate being in a vehicle that you are not controlling. Buy a car, you say. Now you are dependent on your income to control your anxiety. The specter of that angst is hovering above your employment.

These are simple examples, with the layers of social pressures or obligations. But the luxury of just not doing something is not easily there. Desensitization means forgoing your personal agency and feeling, and supplicating to the world. You may get desensitized, but what kind of comfort is it? It is the comfort of having to stand in the same spot for hours on end and locking your knees. You may stay upright. But your legs will hate you.

Drifting away is not an option. Being carried away by the current is.

5.7: Anxious Authors

It is the tendency of the anxious that write books today about anxiety and depression to drift towards mainstream explanations, research, methods, and norms. This is understandable for a couple of reasons.

First, science is good. Facts are good. Research is a positive plan of approach. Measuring and using real examples shows the validity of things. It demonstrates what is real and actual. Some things are inarguable. Objectivity is possible. We should do this when we can.

Second, people want to be a part of the prime narrative. That story affects a person. It shapes their way of thinking because it surrounds them on all sides. The mind naturally is shaped by surroundings, and thinking conforms in a number of ways. Likewise, explanations tend to lean towards the reasoning that is constantly demonstrated in front of a person.

But, anxiety is not objective, as much as we try to make it or believe that it is. It is lived individually. Simultaneously, yes. In concert, yes. But each voice is a single voice, with its own qualities. The measures are all self reported. And the stories are all plotted individually. We should embrace this individuality of anxiety, and do our best to recognize the similarities amongst us. But we also have to be clear that these data points are affected by the observer, who is also affected by the world.

Going deeper is possible. Writing a new story is possible.

5.8: Is Anxiety Good or Necessary in Any Way?

To what extent is anxiety good and necessary?

Is it essential and inescapable?

There is a message out there that says: Anxiety is a normal response. It is a natural reaction to what we encounter. It is instinct.

What we feel from anxiety is not good. It does not feel pleasant. Furthermore, the anxiety in itself does not offer anything positive, unless you ascribe to the idea that the fight or flight response is a true response, passed down over millennia, that protects us from actual danger. Many of us suffering from anxieties and phobias can tell you that what we fear is logically unreasonable and not a threat, so that idea is debatable.

Our reasoning through what we observe, combined with our prior habitual patterns of thinking and values, produce anxiety within us. This anxiety feels bad. It does not serve a purpose. We can derive meaning from it. We can assign a value to it. It does not come with its own weight—we make it heavy.

We can also operate without it. Anxiety does not enrich anything. It does not prevent danger either. There is no higher calling of the feeling of terror. It is the way that we function as embodied humans, for sure, but this "normal" part of being does not equate to something good or necessary.

5.9: Scientific Approaches

We live in a time where there is a backlash against scientific approaches. Facts are being deprioritized. Perhaps they always were, and we are just more attuned to it now that we understand how our own attitudes contribute to actions. The way that we measure the effectiveness of these methods is what should really be questioned.

Do you feel less anxious when you use a pharmaceutical solution? Yes, probably. But at what cost? And is just feeling less anxious than before adequate? To what end is less anxious better? Only to the end that you just need to get on with everything else happening in your day, and just getting the edge off is a low bar to clear. The trade off has to be considered.

Cognitive Behavioral Therapy is about managing, not curing. Is there a cure? What are you trying to cure? It focuses on symptoms and managing them. It is a laser onto the physical and practical side of thought. It is no help when trying to decipher meaning or purpose.

What we end up with is a society that is sensitive to the problems, but ineffective and shallow in addressing them. It is a passing conversation. It is shying away from the big, real issues that we face. What it creates is a constant state of anxiousness, always under the surface. Even when we are able to function at a high level, there is always something lurking just underneath that is not right.

It is unsettling. We are constantly expending energy to keep our balance. The current therapeutic methods are enough to keep us upright. But the headwinds are strong and we bend.

5.10: Pushed

We are pushed back. Back into the middle. Back to society's demands. Back to the rat race. Back to the everyday as it has been. Back to the routine. It is a headwind when we try to break out of it, no doubt.

Why is it that we never get the feeling that the mainstream pushes us forwards? The idea of doing things the normal way or the way that everybody else does it never feels like something that is for our betterment. But, we cannot objectively say that it is unequivocally not. It may just be that we do not notice it. Or, that because it is so commonplace, benefits of the mundane are just more natural and less noticeable. But that would suggest some kind of neutrality, some kind of suspended, in-between state that is neither demeaning nor stimulating–at best.

5.11: Mental Health Day

Mental health days are not enough.

Take one if you need one, right now. But mental health days are short term attempts at course correction that ultimately fall short of meaningful change, even if they are well intentioned. The idea that taking a day for yourself comes with the agreement that you will return the next day, ready to get back to work again as if all is well. Why? Something is not right, and taking a single day off is not going to fix it. It is a method to get us to accept our stressful societal conditions. What is around us does not need to change, it says, when it really does.

We should not want to take them. Most anxious and depressed people that I know, me included, do not want to accept any special considerations. Instead, what if the world changed, rather than making me take a day to not do anything. It is a con to get us to give more. Really we should be examining what we are giving, and change something so that we give differently.

5.12: The Cycle

Therapies are essentially designed today just to get us back into society–the same society that is often the cause of the anxiety. (For the purposes of this discussion, I am moving the cause of anxiety fully outside of the self, even if the anxiety is a reaction that exists within us.) This is not to discount chemical factors. This is not to discount the process that our minds go through constantly, naturally, attempting to make sense of the world. But it is all a reaction to that outside stimulus. That catalyst is the world, which we are simultaneously a part of and separate.

It is a constant cycle. Become anxious, get treatment, feel better, get back out there, start slipping back into anxiety, tune up with the treatment, get back out there, slip back, and on and on. New adages come along the way. New angles are used to address it (is this book all just an angle?). New drugs are used to address it. New dosages. New combinations. New therapies. Have you heard about the things that they are doing with psychedelics?

All of it is just to get you back into the life around you though, and not about your agency beyond getting into the cycle. There can be more, I am convinced. I do not think that anyone would disagree, but they are intimidated, so it is not their goal. Their goal is to get you back into the water, floating with your head just above, like a buoy, bobbing.

5.13: Stigma, Again

Anxiety equals weakness. That is the stigma. Not being able to do what you want when you want is a show that you are not in control, and are not as "good" as someone else that can impose their will on and within a situation.

Society favors the strong. Those that can take for themselves and are fully self-reliant are valorized. The killer instinct pervades our popular culture: it is masculine. It is machismo made real. It is winning to the extreme.

Anxiety represents a failure, you think. A deficiency. After all, you should be able to soar. You should be able to do the great things that you see depicted on television, or on your smartphone. You should be without fear. Acknowledgement of your own nervousness serves to show your authenticity, provided you overcome it, and move on. Consider examples of people that have mentioned their anxiety. Now they are labeled. Now it is always in the back of everyone's mind.

Here is the truth: what is in the back of everyone's mind is the same as the front: their own anxieties. They encounter the conflicts of the mind themselves and do what they can to make sense of it all, to act to make it stop. Often, it is at the expense of others. The rest of us. Rather than try to eliminate anxiety, they try to move on from their own.

5.14: Options

In a universe that is indifferent to us, there are three options.

The middle option is just try to go along and do the best we can. It is sometimes annoying, sometimes tolerable, sometimes miserable. It is the option of auto-pilot that is one day interrupted by panic. Most therapies today try to get us back to that mode. To get along.

On the poles are two other options. One is akin to a Buddhist way of thinking. It is accepting our insignificance and allowing the world to guide us. It is an openness to what is thrown at us and adapting, accepting. New age philosophies are not dissimilar.

The other option is to fight it. To rebel. To attempt to shape the world to our will.

Both of these polar options have their pluses and minuses. In the way of full acceptance, you are totally at the will of something outside of you. There is little to no conversation. You are fully floating while the waves move you to where they say you should be. The world guides. We hope it is to somewhere good. Or, in the sway of raging waters, you swim, even though the waves may thrash you. You may get to be where you want to be, though.

5.15: Acceptable Behavior

There is a fire in a person's house because they left a clothes iron on unattended. Nobody was hurt and damage was minor, but from then on, the person is fearful of it happening again. They are so afraid of it happening again that they now never use an iron, only a steamer.

Even if someone thinks that anxiety is unreasonable, I do not believe that anyone would argue that the reactive behavior above needs to be changed. The person will just go on the rest of their lives not using an iron and getting wrinkles out of their clothes with the steamer. We can think of other examples where a person's thoughts, whether the result of a trauma or not, affect their behavior in a way that is either pure avoidance, outside of what we would normally expect a person to do, or at worst destructive.

Behavior as the result of a neurosis may be unnoticeable. Some acts at a small scale may get a side-eyed response. At a next level, we might ask into it, looking for an explanation that is perhaps more rooted in the real world that we share or relate to. If more extreme, we may clash with it. At a certain point, it requires some kind of treatment.

What are the benchmarks between a quirk and problem? A standard for intervention seems to be if the anxiety interrupts your normal day or prevents you from doing what you are supposed to do on a given day. This is problematic because it ascribes what a standard day is like, and also establishes it as something that should not be detoured from. A person anxious about work should always go to work, is what this can be boiled down to. If you are afraid of public transportation but have to use it to get around town, it should not be avoided. Imagine even more generalized situations. Indeed, the idea is that you should not leave the stream of existence that has been set up.

This response from our society and professionals in the field asks us to ignore what our own minds tell us. It de facto says that our own interpretations of the world are wrong. When you are already full of angst, living in a confused state of stress that you want to avoid but it will not avoid you, delegitimizing the thoughts that you have is disorienting. It is a diagnosis of malfunctioning, when in fact, you are functioning exactly as you are supposed to be, albeit with a result that is uncomfortable and personally painful.

But why is the person that swears off irons acceptable, but the person that wants to swear off travel in need of therapy? How come the teen depressed with their home life is asked to look at the bright side rather than finding a way to make things better? Why is the person unhappy with their life given a prescription, and not a better way to live? Why is the precipice from acceptable to unacceptable at either a point of comfort for *others,* or orbiting around whether or not you are able to contribute to society?

An anxious person is already feeling around for themselves, as they have encountered a conflict between what they think they should be as a person and what they are experiencing and being told that they are. The response to it is far too often to subjugate it even further. Turn this on its head. Your mind is doing what it does. It is not wrong. It is reasoning. It is, actively, making sense. It has found a part of the world that requires change.

Chapter 6

6.1: Not Worth It

It is not worth it. I do not think I am telling you anything that you do not already know. It is not worth getting anxious over all these things. They are all fleeting and light. And I do not mean that just because of the transitory nature of our day. Life itself–the world and our existence–is not worth getting worked up over if we recognize its meaninglessness and absurdity. Right?

If you want to know how bad smoking is for you, ask a smoker. Likewise, if you want to know how futile anxiety is, ask someone with an anxiety disorder. Even though the anxiety is a natural outgrowth of our thinking, it serves no purpose. How could it? It cannot warn against something, as there is nothing to actually warn against. It cannot steer us in a certain direction, because the world is directionless. Anxiety is useless and that is perhaps the most frustrating part of it: the pointlessness that we are burdened with.

What we have is a dichotomy of worthlessness. If

the world is without meaning and our anxiety is without meaning, where does that leave us? Ultimately, the speech I have to give, that is making me sick with nerves, is not important to the universe. My disappointment with my life does not matter to the world. The unease I feel when I wake up is not noticed by existence. Ultimately, even if my worst fears come to bear, it is insignificant in the grand scheme of things.

I can say all of these things to myself, yet I am still anxious. I can remind myself of the emptiness of everything, yet I still worry. I can think of the arbitrariness of my context, and it still saddens me. With the meaninglessness, now enters what appears to be powerlessness. It is depressing, yes–that is what it is, that is how they are all so close to each other. My anxiety simply exists–meaningless amongst indifference. That is just the way that it is. The worthlessness of everything is all consuming. That is just the way that I feel. Here is the deepest point of hopelessness. Even knowing the truth of it, my mind still does what it does, and I am not strong enough to change the cycle that it runs.

At least it feels that way.

6.2: Is There a Moral Reaction?

It is easy to believe that nobody wants to be anxious. It feels like hell, and the circumstances in which someone would choose actual distress and despair are hard to imagine. From that view alone, we can say that we are anti-anxiety.

Is there a moral reaction that we should have towards anxiety? To our own anxiety? To the anxiety of others?

Anxiety in itself does not require a moral reaction. There are no obligations within the feeling. Any reaction would be based on a moral obligation that one has towards suffering or the negative in general.

Seeing others suffer elicits a consistent feeling of moral obligation. We see someone suffering or sense that they are uneasy and we feel the need to comfort them. It is in our nature, and most would say that it is something that we should do. Morally, it is "good" to both reduce someone's suffering on an individual level, and more globally to reduce negative feelings. It is arguable whether or not someone has to do this, or rather, if they do nothing at all they are somehow doing something bad. In that way, saying that there is a moral obligation to reduce others' anxiety seems like an over-prescription. But when we zoom out and say plainly that anxiety is something negative, it becomes more apparent where we should stand.

How we address it morally becomes interesting. We can soothe a person by rubbing their back, by saying "It'll be OK," or by offering a glass of water. These are all normal, banal things we do when we have someone in front of us that is panicking. But we also know from personal experience that much of this is insufficient, to say the least. So how can we do better? We can address the source: identifying what is causing the anxiety and reducing it from peoples' lives, eliminating it if possible, makes obvious sense. When the anxiety—or the cause of the anxiety—is more generalized, the way that we combat it, and what we combat, must be bigger. Let us deal with the general, ethereal anxiety that so many feel: if modernity is the culprit, consider what should be done. Consider the change that is necessary. There are other massive anxious accelerators out there. If there is an obligation to act, the obligation is far reaching. This is a large, scary, call to action. I get nervous just typing it. I feel the shake in my body. But if we recognize the collective despair, we can also recognize how it feels on an individual level.

To our own anxiety, though, any moral component seems to disappear. What *must* I do about my own anxiety, morally? We don't often talk about moral obligations to ourselves, and anxiety in itself does not offer an additional path to it. So why beat it? That is up to you, I suppose.

6.3: You May Think This Is All Building to Something

You may think that this is all building to something. *That is what we do.* Do you get it by now? We believe that everything is building to something. Our mind creates that story. It all must have a plot, we think. It starts, there is a middle, and it ends in some kind of crescendo that ties it all up nicely. This book must as well. Physically, in front of you, you know that there are a finite number of pages. It must lead to somewhere.

But it does not. At least I do not know if it really does. I have some ideas. They are mostly restating and reframing other things. It is a different perspective, I hope. But it is not an end. Anxiety has no end. Our stories have no end. The stories of our lives have a finite end, but it is not one of resolution. The lessons learned do not mean some kind of application or denouement. And that is even if lessons are learned. If they are, do they stick? Do they stay around forever? Do they get overtaken by other things, and we need new methods to be able to survive? Funny how the anxiety seems to find a way and our adages do not.

There is no Great Insight. A unified theory of everything. That climax, that panacea, does not really exist in life. We have always known this in some way. That is the absurdity. The hopelessness. Ask Camus. Ask Kierkegaard. Not only is the world uncaring, but it is also without reason. There is no point. That shark staring back at us does not remember us. The thing that we are chasing is totally indifferent to us.

This is a book that is written. Of course, deliberately, I am doing my best to create some sort of climax or resolution. But it is not a natural one, as much as I would like it to be. It is my construction. My reasoning. It is my mind trying to make sense of anxiety, trying to explain it, and in doing so, disarming it, eliminating it.

Which, as I said above, is impossible.

6.4: It's Getting Heavy

It's getting heavy.

When we say that something is "getting heavy" we do not mean that it is gaining weight. We mean that we are weakening. We project ourselves onto that thing outside of us. Likewise, the world wears us out. We tire from it.

6.5: Minimization

We try to minimize our anxieties, when we maybe should be minimizing that thing that we are anxious about. Many schools of thought and methods do this today when they ask us to consider the likelihood of our fears coming true, or what that would really look like. It is an attempt to call the bluff of our fears. What it ignores is how much the anxiety itself is torture. You may battle through it, but it still feels terrible. The intent is to show that you can still accomplish your goal on the other side of the anxiety, but oftentimes that negative experience can only serve to reinforce the nervousness and fear associated with it. A sense of accomplishment is dwarfed by a sense of exhausted relief.

The spiritual approach almost shifts the focus from

the internal to the external when it asks us to be in concert with the world outside of us.

To some extent there are things that we must accept. I cannot do anything about a meteorite screaming towards the Earth. The serenity prayer, accepting things that you cannot change and all, is the most trite example of this. It is like a psychological or epistemological golden rule—a cousin to the categorical imperative. This does not make the reality of annihilation by a space rock any less scary to us, or likely.

6.6: Attitudes

There are points when our minds tell us that we should or must feel anxious. It is an odd feeling. You encounter a situation where you consciously realize that it is the same or similar to other times when you experienced anxiety. But it is not at a point of dread, or maybe just is not quite as intense. Nonetheless, your mind sees that starting line. It may walk you up to it. It shows you a finish line: panic.

Similarly, there are situations where parts of our environment or consumption tell us that we should feel anxious about something. This can be relentless, with urgent language and scary persistence.

These attitudes towards the world and the self ("You should be anxious," a voice tells you) remove your agency. They remove your ability to decipher and control yourself. That is not to say that it is easy. But it also allows predetermination originating from non-divine locations to lord over you. There is no god of anxiety. Or, if there is one, Oizys, Miseria, she is not of this world and ethereal.

6.7: If Society Is a Cause

If society is a cause of anxiety—the pressures, the expectations, the social constructs—do we have an imperative to change society? In an age of oppressiveness, with many suffering, what must we do?

Unless we accept a moral imperative, we are not required to do anything. However, if we want change, we do not have to limit ourselves to self-care or self-improvement. For fair reasons, therapy focuses on the individual in the chair, and the skills for coping. But there is power, for the self and for the world at large, in aiming towards our surroundings, instead of limiting ourselves to an inward, often accusatory, gaze which can be distracting and self-defeating.

6.8: They Say That Anxiety Is Natural

They say anxiety is natural and we need it. It is inherited from our ancient ancestors, keeping us safe from danger. As if our ancestors knew danger before they encountered it. They believe fears are inborn in us, there before we ever encounter the predators, the ocean abyss, or the absence of others. The fear protects us from these possible realities as a natural human governor, they say.

No, we do not need anxiety. But we have it. A fight or flight response may be driven by a shot of adrenaline and other physiological factors. But psychically, what good does it do? How does it help us, other than making us act fast? It makes us skip steps in our thinking. It does not allow integration. It launches us as we jump to conclusions, which may or may not happen, and may or may not be reasonable.

6.9: Obsession

Our feelings are insignificant in the scheme of things. Our anxiety is irrelevant to the world. Still, we obsess over things that, when we step back in our perspective, do not matter.

But, they are significant to us. They have meaning for us. They point to other meanings. Anxiety is a precursor. A herald. It announces to us what we do not yet know clearly. But it is no less present.

We obsess over anxiety because we know that it holds a truth, even though it is not logical, even though it deals in things that are not facts. It still trades in something that is real to us. The future that it portends is as real as any other future. Likely or not, it talks of possibility, just like any possibility. It cannot be ignored because that would mean ignoring ourselves.

We obsess over ridding ourselves of anxiety because it does not comply. It is perhaps the loudest and least ignorable part of our automatic underlying thoughts. It stretches from that place that functions without the deliberateness that we can exert.

We obsess over it because it is so foreign, yet so familiar. It is confusing, but makes sense.

6.10: The Personally Absurd

When we talk about the absurd, we often describe a truth of humanity—a shared experience—that is the opposite of what we collectively think should be the case. While what we explain may be relatable and fully understandable, a single human or societal perception does not exist. All perceptions are individual, and while they may add up to a collective idea, each piece is subjective.

Always, it is personally absurd. We each find an experience to be in conflict with what we want, or think that it should be. We think that there should be meaning in the world. We think that what we value should be valued, and respected, by all. While the details may differ, the experience is the same. You may think that everyone should abhor violence in all forms. I may be concerned that we do not emphasize our shared health adequately. Neither of us may disagree with the other, even if our hierarchy of values is different. Both of us, though, are unfulfilled by the world around us and recognize that the world does not, and may never, be what we think it should be. Yet we cannot shake our fears. The absurdity is personal.

When the oppressiveness of the world, or even our

more acute surroundings, becomes unbearable, we recognize the absurdity that we all share. The variety of the absurdities only emphasizes the meaninglessness of our personal existential conflicts. As part of the world, we are both a victim of the absurdity and absurd ourselves–expecting something when there is nothing, crying to be rescued and simultaneously acting the antagonist to ourselves, others, and the world itself.

If we recognize this power, we may unlock a new agency and a way to rebel against the anxiety that springs from the absurd conflict between the world and ourselves.

Chapter 7

7.1: Anxiety Is a Clearing

Anxiety is a clearing. It shows the incongruence of the self and the world, and when we understand the ability of the self to apply meaning in a meaningless world, we gain power to live how we please. We apply the meaning–if we take the opportunity to.

Existing where the conflict in our mind grows, anxiety stretches its arms to its sides, pushing everything else to the margins, eventually to irrelevance, until only anxiety remains. The anxiety becomes the fear itself.

But anxiety does not have to be the primary resident. It clears out a space, but must not always occupy it. Anxiety shows that what lives there is changeable. It is adjustable. It is optional. And while anxiety may be difficult to evict, it is not inevitable and it does not have to be permanent.

7.2: Why Should the Self Always Come Second to the World

We can change ourselves.

We try to change all of the time. It is not always easy. We are pushed to change. Mantras and overused phrases, like "become your best self," "bettering myself," and "in a state of becoming," dominate parts of the zeitgeist. "Improve!" we are commanded. You must get better. You must change what you are, who you are. I ask: why me? Why us? Why must we be the ones to change, when it is the world that should change? Why are we the ones to change?

We can only change ourselves so much. And why should the self always be burdened by the world? Indeed, just as we are always changing in some way, the world is as well. But to what end? And for what purpose? Many of the ways that we experience the changing of the world are determined by forces outside of us. Changes to our immediate world can happen: I can buy a new desk, I can drink a different kind of soda, I can replace my reading glasses. But there is a mass of the world that we cannot just as easily change. In fact, the world will actively resist that change. Perhaps it feels like it will laugh at our attempts. Truly, it is totally indifferent to them.

To what extent is this part of the world other people? A significant portion—which tells us something: it is actually just as susceptible to change. Changing the world, in large part, is changing other people. So do not be afraid of it. Push back, for yourself.

But remember, they are also selfs.

For the parts that are automatic, that others take for granted, we must work harder. We do not have to just accept. We do not have to be second. Why should we? Why does the world always have to win?

7.3: Change

The world needs to change. Do not let them tell you it is you. Simply changing your perspective will only go so far.

Changing the world starts by assigning the meaning that we want. What means something to us. What is most important. What do we want. Find what should change. Do not stop when the world tells you what or how something is supposed to be. You decide. Have that agency.

The world, society, culture, and others, dictate to us what is important: what must be. Our thinking adopts this. It molds around it. It is not always what we actually want or need. This conflict brings about anxiety. It makes us anxious when something does not fit within ourselves. Our mind is trying to make it right, but it cannot. It is having a hard time making sense of it.

So change it.

You can, and will, change your thinking. But you should change it to change the world. Changing just to tolerate the world will lead to an infinite fight with the unending, relentless pressure that it applies. The world asks you to resign yourself. Your mind, through its awesome ability to reason, sees patterns, connects dots, and takes joy in those realizations. It cannot help but acquiesce. But we are more than that. We have competing thoughts, including our sense of self and the way that we think things should be.

Change the world, be an agent, and feel better. The world does not hold a monopoly on what should be or how things should be. You can decide what is important to you.

7.4: A Clearing

My anxiety was a clearing. I have survived with anxiety, and with that survival I have seen what is necessary and what is not. I have seen the reasons and what is really all for not. Everything that I was supposed to do, and ways that I was supposed to feel, did not affect my survival. In fact, those things that I missed because of anxiety have melted into simply other options, not things that I had to do.

The things that I am afraid of, which I feel that I have to or had to do, I see now that the necessity was self imposed–a relic of a world that told me what was important and what was not. I stopped fighting my anxiety and I listened to it, tried to understand what it was saying. It told me of the conflict between what I wanted and what the world wanted. There was a conflict of what I thought should be versus what was. And when I gave into the anxiety in my mind, I did not stop. I did not succumb to the hopelessness or the despair. I did not stop at the meaninglessness of it all. Rather, the breakdown of reason was an opening for me to build it back to what I wanted. It is an unstable structure, sure. But I am luckier than others. I think of them often. I know them. I am them.

There are no reasons. No reason to fight my anxiety. No reason to explore it. No reason to pull deeper meaning from the anxiety itself. No reason for anything, no reason to do anything. The world is not prescriptive. The (natural) universe is the clearing, and it gives no direction.

For too long the personal agency to fill this void has been suppressed, taken from us, wherever it can be. History makes demands on us. Our society hides options other than its own. Do you see? They are usurpers.

7.5: Get Through the Day

An amazing amount of what we do is just to get through the day. We do this at the most basic of levels, like being able to eat or have shelter, for ourselves or for others that we believe depend on us. In other ways, it is more about emotional survival or instinct. A piece of us goes with the flow—the flow that we were born into and carried along with as we became older. We demonstrate this through actions, but it originates elsewhere.

Our thinking, for instance, is no different. Our minds want to get along. They are programmed to do that. It acts like, or maybe just is, instinct. Our mind cruises through situations, intuiting next steps and reaching conclusions. Most are innocuous and banal, as much of life is, but what the brain is doing in these situations remains just as outstanding as when we are conscious of our thinking. Perhaps it is even more amazing on its own, on that sub-aware level.

We seek out things to help us get through the day. What can make my day easier? Maybe it is prepared meals. Or laying out outfits. Or adjusting our schedule. All of these are methods that people use to reduce stress.

When you have anxiety, the options, and needs, change. Medications and therapies certainly help. Meditation is something that people use. Routine certainly helps you make it through.

Is getting through the day enough, though? Maybe. What is "getting through"? What is the measure of success there? Is it just survival? It is if you say it is. But you have to say it. You have to be the judge of your success.

When someone is evaluated for an anxiety disorder, one thing a professional asks is whether or not they are able to get up, get out of bed, and go to their job. In other words, is it difficult to get through the day?

Who is to say?

Well, you, of course.

Who else can decide if you had a difficult time or not? Who else can say whether you enjoyed it or were tortured? There is certainly an objective piece to this—I can tell whether you enjoyed something or not by your reaction. However, that is through you. A rock may be impossible for you to lift, but that judgment is only made when considering you. Now, imagine that a rock is not absurdly large, and I cannot tell whether or not it is too heavy for you to lift. In fact, you can get it off the ground. You can lift it, but almost immediately you say, "This is too much!" and let it fall back to the earth. You lifted it. It was not too heavy. But you recognized your limit. Perhaps someone else could have endured it for longer.

Imagine it is not a rock but stress. I cannot tell whether or not something is stressful enough to cause you anxiety. But you can—either by enduring it and exhibiting your reaction, or by communicating it.

Most of life is just getting through the day. It is just bearably being on autopilot. It is not always hard, or, we do not want it to always be hard. It should not have to be. We should be able to coast. It should be automatic. Our perception of it all should be automatic. There does not have to be struggle.

7.6: Rebellion Everyday

We rebel. The everyday is simultaneously terrifying and boring, so we try to break out. We try to add some spice, some excitement. We try to break up the monotony. We correct the banal wrongs we deal with every day.

If we string these together, rebellions can become the new normal. Incorporating these acts into our routine can create a new routine. It is like exercising–creating muscle memory.

Consider that our expectations and how we perceive the world are shaped by the way that we think. If we add to it, augment it, create our own new steps—we are shaping it, and can change the way that we think, and change what we find meaningful. The effect, hopefully, is to overall reduce the conflict in our minds, reduce anxiety.

The key is rebellion, though. Something different. Change. Getting used to something miserable and anxiety inducing does not improve your situation.

When thinking situates itself around rebellion, the rebellion lives in thinking. What is expected has changed, and hopefully, it is something better. The anxiety may not completely melt away, but it is not where it was before. Instead, a different type of mental reaction has taken root. Real estate taken up by anxiety is now occupied by new reasonings, imaginations, and meanings.

7.7: There Is Something Bigger Than You

There is something bigger than you. You can focus on the fact that you are so small, if you want. You can have the perspective that you are but a spec of sand in the universe, smaller than that even, and your contribution to the greatness of the universe is so infinitesimal that it is worth nothing. You can also recoil in horror from the enormity of that which is outside of you.

At times, we all do these things, how can you not? But we do not have to react this way.

The sublimity of the universe can fill us with awe rather than dread.

The nothingness and meaningless of it all is a place for you to play. It is an eternal return to anything you see fit.

7.8: Imagination

Imagine knowing the answers.

Imagine everything making sense.

We know that this is impossible. We know that we do not know everything, whether that be because of the vastness and volume of everything there is in the world, or our time and place that bounds what is knowable in the moment.

Nevertheless, we try. We try not just consciously sometimes, but we try subconsciously *all the time.* We take in information. Process it. Connect dots. We cannot have all of the information—we cannot know all of the reasons—but we put it all together anyways. Our imagination takes over. And it can be sublime.

When our minds try to make sense of the world,

they do not have every single piece of information. They try to fill in the gaps. If those gaps cannot be filled in, or what slides into place is terrifying, we find anxiety. But, if our imagination runs from one thought to the other, solving little mysteries and uncovering secrets in our mind, it is at play. It makes us feel alive.

We encounter this all of the time when we consume media. It is when we daydream. It is why some people are drawn in to gossip and planning vacations. It is also why some engage with conspiracy theories.

Our imagination is a mechanism for play or anxiety. Which it is depends on what came before–what informs our minds and programs our imaginations. All of the possibilities of what can and cannot be are opportunities to be anxious or excited. You must engage with the positive possibilities of your imaginations. It is visualization. It is modeling. It is pretending. It is playing.

7.9: The World Has No Meaning

The world has no meaning, we see now. So we can apply our own.

There may be things in the way of this power. It may be difficult to see the path. Is it a path? Or is it more of a "place that is no longer in the through part"? There are lures to stay here. Like sirens, but stationary. Like whatever power held Sisyphus to his task. Camus imagines a Sisyphus that smiles–that is his addition to the story. If we are going to change it, let us change it: Sisyphus can walk free. He can let the rock go, and let it roll away.

We adapt stories all of the time. We make interpretations of our own. We draw conclusions and bend to our purposes. It should not be any different this time. Narratives are malleable and we make them. They exist from us, from within us. Think of the lyric, "The sun will come up, tomorrow." It is a statement, yet we inherently hear ideas of hope and new beginnings in the words. That is not in the words, though. The sun *will* come up tomorrow, as it does every day, we intuit. We have been the receiver of enough other information, stories, plots, media, and pictures to create this kind of cause-and-effect that immediately connects the idea and image of the sun rising for a new day with a new spiritual beginning of sorts, with new beginnings and new chances for success and joy.

The dawn is meaningless. It happens, daily. It literally *is* daily. But we apply meaning to the idea itself. Why stop there?

It is not easy to create, and to create when so much else does it. But we can.

This example is symbolic. The sun. Hope. New beginnings. Possibility! But there are more practical applications as well. We apply meaning to tasks we do every day, to interactions with other people, to our meals, to holidays. Consider the flag of your nation. The clothes you wear. Mementos in your drawers. You have applied many of these meanings. The world around you and society has applied others and you have gone along. You see the possibility here?

7.10: Facts and Truths

Facts are not enough. Your fears cannot be placated simply by statements. You are afraid of ghosts. I can tell you that ghosts do not exist—we have no evidence of them. But that is not enough. What we believe, the stories that we tell ourselves, the algorithms that run in our mind, the ways that we think, are not fully based on factual information. We cannot reason with our fears. We know that they are unreasonable. But we have ways that we can deal with the unreasonable.

Think about the world and its indifference to our feelings. The facts of our surroundings do not care about our feelings. In fact, many of the facts do not care about each other. But, do not tell our minds that. We draw connections. We make the meanings. Into something else. Something we believe in. The results are not always good, of course. We have established that.

The lines are drawn and the loyalties are clear.

We reason through the world. This is how we live. We get into trouble when we try to reason *with* the world. The world does not always want to be reasoned with. We can go ahead and try, but at certain points, we have to move on.

Because the facts are not enough, we can use what we have—our feelings, our desires, our own reasonings–to fill the gaps. Plenty of parts of the world and society try to do this. And we allow them. It is easier. But it often clashes with what we would use. Again, anxiety persists here.

Imagine that you instead impose your will. Your truth. Meshing that with the world. Making the connections that you need to make in order to create the full world the way that you would have it, making yourself into an existence that you want.

It is partly survival. We make sense of it all, so that we can go on. But what if we can go further? What if we can thrive? What if that were possible? The anxiety is there, but we move on from it, through our own truths, that we impose on the world.

7.11: What Is the Point When All There Were Before Are Gone?

You should make things matter because you can. It is a tremendous opportunity, afforded to us all, that we do not recognize in our daily, autopilot, thinking-without-having-to-think lives.

Make something out of nothing.

In front of you is a pile of kindling. In your hand is a lit torch. It is cold outside. *Light the fire.* Our brains beg for meaning. We search for it in everything, whether we do so purposely or not. It is involuntary, like breathing. If all meaning is gone, and we thirst for it, for ourselves we must make it.

But it does not have to be an involuntary and base

exercise. It does not have to be perfunctory or utilitarian. With the ability to choose is an ability to play. To enjoy. To decide on something that we like, that feels right.

The point is to make it better for ourselves. Now what is better for each of us will be different, and that emphasizes why it is important to find the meaning for ourselves. As much as we may even be dedicated to others or a greater good, that is still just a framework by which we ourselves find our own meaning. If I feel that it is right for me to be selfless in a situation, my meaning is still derived from that situation. Even if I do something for another person, it fits within my thought process, meaning applied, and sense-making. It is not an anxious situation, as my mind is congruent, it is at play, seeing how my actions contribute to something "larger"–within myself as it may actually be.

7.12: Implications

There is no meaning but that which we make. So, is it nihilism? Hedonism? Some kind of moral relativism? I am not so sure.

Firstly, just because everything has no inherent meaning, it does not mean that all meaning that we find applied by forces outside of us is negative. We may decide, for ourselves, that some of it is good. Traditions are not necessary, but they are not to be eschewed for no reason. We can enjoy them. We can like them. We can think that they are good to carry on. They can make us better.

Better for what? That brings in the second point: if we recognize our own agency in determining what does and does not matter, we must also recognize that ability of others. Do you choose to respect that right? I suppose it is situational. If that right and the meaning applied from it does not conflict with your own meaning, you will be comfortable allowing it. But if it clashes with your meaning, and your beliefs, then you will not be as amenable to what they think is important.

For example: At Thanksgiving your family gets together and you have your traditional meal with turkey, potatoes, cranberry sauce, and other special side dishes unique to your celebration. It is special to you and the tradition has meaning to you and your family. Likewise, your neighbors have their own unique meal for Thanksgiving. Neither is less important to each family. The variety is great. Neither is better or worse than the other.

Imagine another scenario where you believe that the ocean is essentially sacred. As the majority of the earth's surface, it should be protected at all costs, for its ecological value, for the inhabitants of it, and for your own enjoyment. Now there also may be a person that owns a factory. The factory makes chemicals important for medical laboratory experiments, however, the manufacturing of these chemicals produces a significant amount of waste. The owner of the factory, who believes strongly in their mission to help with these important medical experiments, has no problem allowing his toxic waste to drain into the ocean. The ocean holds no meaning to them. So whose meaning wins? Are you supposed to suppress your meaning for theirs? Do you respect what they find meaningful or not meaningful?

Of course not.

This clash can hopefully be resolved through reasoning and looking for shared, base values. It may also call for one to stand steadfast and act in ways to protect what they find meaningful. These are choices that we must make and use our judgment for throughout our lives. Nonetheless, for our conversation, it is good that you do in fact have something that is valuable to you.

Having a meaning, especially one that you choose and embrace, is the giant step. A step in the right direction—a step that feels right, a step towards feeling right. It is putting all of our weight on the earth, and using it to go where we want to go. But watch out. With meaning, our moving feet, the earth below, and the world around us, shifts are always possible and a conflict is always lurking. The incongruence and collapse—harbingers of anxiety and depression—are never inactive. We must each just be better than them, and each choose better.

7.13: Their Meaning

All of the measurements, all of the warning signs, all of the data points, all of the symptoms, and all of the treatments are *their* meanings. They are statements on what it means to be not anxious–"normal"–in the world. They are parts of strategies designed to get you back towards contributing to their own goals and desires.

It is often asked if your anxiety is disrupting your day-to-day, if it is disrupting your ability to go to work. Work holds meaning to whoever is asking that question. What is perhaps more apt to ask is: is your anxiety disrupting you from doing anything that you *really want to do*? How does it mesh with what you think you should be doing?

That requires an examination of what you think you should be doing, which in itself should be informative and help identify what does and does not mean something to you. The result, though, is being able to communicate and act on what does mean something to you, and orient yourself towards that, not what outside forces determine has meaning.

If none of what you are supposed to be doing has a purpose to you, you do not have to gauge how you feel based on it. You can live your life according to what does have meaning to you, and not cause angst pursuing what does not.

7.14: Our Minds Want to Find Meaning and Reason

Our minds want to find meaning and reason. Why is the sky blue? Why is there something instead of nothing? Is there a God? What is the meaning of life? What is the purpose of this? Why did you do that? What is happening?

Why am I this way?

Our natural state is one of sensing, taking in, perceiving, and arranging that information into something that forms a story–like a string–for us to follow. Perhaps to believe in. It is how we move through the world and how we function. That we are able to do this so automatically is nothing short of wonderful as human beings.

When something does not fit right, or the story it tells disagrees with another story that we have, we have a problem. Anxiety lives.

But how does the anxiety make sense? That is why we examine it. That is why we ask where it came from. Because it is what we do. We need to know why. That is why I cannot just be content to not go on an elevator, or not swim in water over my head. Or get married. Or leave the house. Or be content. Because we need to understand why those things are not for us. Maybe we will find that they are for us, just in a way that we did not recognize. Or maybe we just find what makes us unique, and accept that we do not conform to those notions.

We rationalize everything, whether we try or not. Some things are harder than others. Anxiety happens to be harder because it shows where there are challenges in our existing understandings, of the world, and of ourselves.

7.15: Ego Riff

The world has no meaning. So we apply it. But why? And *what*?

To nourish our egos. I say that as a statement about our own selves and our senses of it. It is not that we are all egotistical.

Imagine someone is afraid of traveling, and does not want to, ever. But when they think about who they are, how they consider themselves, or who they want to be, they like to think of themselves as worldly. See that conflict: two opposing parts of the self. If one manifests itself more in the world (their fear of travel, and thus not traveling), an anxious conflict is created by them. If the other manifests (that is, living out their desire to be of the world), their choices and agency manifested are in line with what they think of themselves. Easier said than done, of course, but you see how this goes.

Interestingly, it gives some commentary on who is anxious. Consider the melancholy, the meek, the sensitive–you know the type. You maybe are the type. They have reduced the importance of their selves, which is not necessarily a bad thing in moderation, but they are not what they think they should be, and instead are living as another self that does not represent where they believe that they should be within the world. I am not saying that all people with these traits are depressed. But you see the continuum.

Run this against the "alphas" of the world. All ego. Their consideration for others appears to be much more suppressed in favor of the self. We do not often see them as anxious. It could just be what we see, of course. But if that is the case, consider what it is that we see instead: some type of self-centered, egomaniacal narcissist.

Is there anyone with anxiety and depression that does not seek to understand it, or themselves? We know instinctively that it exists in what we know the most intimately: ourselves. We should know it, we think. We should be able to understand it and control it. Sure, it does not have a simple explanation that can be confirmed through tests at a lab. But no one just wants to take a pill, even if they wish it were that easy to solve, and are content with pharmaceutical attempts at solutions.

Do not mistake the above as a conscious choice. One does not choose between their ego or their anxieties consciously. In fact, each fulfills and strengthens its own position in a way. Ego breeds more ego, to difficult extremes. Anxiety contributes to a loss of nerve and an incongruence with the self. The stories that the ego tells, that it stars in, must be maintained. Likewise, the anxious story becomes the familiar one, becoming like a script that we stand and perform in front of the world. Why one starts or slides one way or the other is like asking what gives a person a certain personality? Nature or nurture? Why not both?

It is a constant exercise of choosing which desires to act upon, and each of those choices feed a different aspect of ourselves. It may reinforce who we are. It may succumb to our fears. What we are is always morphing because of what we choose to make real in the world, and what has meaning.

7.16: Versus

We live within conflict, that we do our best to reconcile.

Theoretical versus real. Ideas versus people. Our inner world versus our outer world.

Different strategies of resolution often favor one side over the other. Goals are different and goals shift. Although focused on our minds, some strategies situate it within a world, which it prioritizes. It seeks to minimize the inner conflict–the anxiety–that we feel, and all too often not actually address the piece that we are missing, that would help us feel whole in the story that we tell about ourselves.

These dichotomies can also lead to cultural anxiety: a world on edge.

7.17: Sublime / Whales

Not everything can be reasoned out, though. Not everything is reasonable. Not everything is *of* reason.

Some things are some of the above. Some are all.

Consider the whale. A gigantic whale. Majestic. Sublime. So obviously more than you or me. In its way, you do not stand a chance. Think of the possibilities.

But whales are not humans. We cannot communicate with them. We cannot have a conversation with them. We cannot reason with them.

Consider also the other situations or even people that we encounter every day that cannot be reasoned with. In turn, we must adapt. We must absorb the situation and do our best to bend it towards the ends that we think should happen. Perhaps we also consider the means. But that is for another time. We are not all powerful. With many situations, though, we can have an effect.

The whale, though, is almost beyond that reason. We can avoid it. Steer around it. But it is not reasonable, at least not in the sense that we live by. It may have a code, or a way of behaving. People today certainly do their best to explain them. But not everything can be explained. Not everything allows itself to be explained.

There is this step further. It is that which is outside of reason. Beyond it. We try to make sense of it. Attempt to make it fit into some type of worldview. But despite our best efforts, it is still just out of reach.

It is greater than us, and what we are able to do. It is at a place where possibility abounds. It can be negative. It can also be positive. It is a place where beauty lives. It has been called the sublime. It is the ultimate unknowable. And it is often bridged with faith.

Our minds try to know everything. They try to comprehend and process everything that they encounter. Sometimes it is easy and we do not even notice it. Sometimes it creates a collision in us, and anxiety springs forth. It is a sunrise that announces to you that it is a new day. It is also a sunset that reminds you of the end of the world.

Even with the sublime, we can choose how to take it, if we do not let it overcome us. Awesomeness works that way. The whale is either our titan savior, or our leviathan doom.

7.18: But This Is Not Easy

But this is not easy. It is difficult to not focus on the day-to-day doldrums of symptom management, talking about how your misery will end, and minimizing the impact. Realize that instead you can rearrange the world–to apply your own meaning to it. We are not comfortable with that power. Are we afraid of it? Are we unsure how to use it?

It seems as though we do not believe–or have not fully internalized and made part of our own thought process–our own ability to shape what we think and in turn the world around us. This is particularly the case for people with anxiety. The world, and how we perceive it, we believe to be in charge. We are convinced, on a subconscious level, that we are fully at the mercy of other forces that are not of our volition.

That being said, it is not as easy as just saying these things to bring them to life. Repeating a mantra over and over every morning before getting out of bed is probably not sufficient either. So what is? Practice. Habituation. Changes in behavior. Commitment to the idea that you have control over these things. Over yourself.

Along with that should come understanding—understanding that it is not as easy as just manifesting it through speech, or even just a single thought. Anxiety, and the world it springs forth from, is strong. It can crush you. It is dead weight that collapses onto you. Flailing will not get you free. Solid footing, on the other hand, with a supported push, can let you move it.

7.19: Why We Feel the Need to Defeat Anxiety

We feel the need to overcome anxiety for two reasons. First it is because the world outside of us, society, and culture tells us to do so. Second, it is because it is in our nature. The first has terrible intentions and places us within a cycle of anxiety. The second is natural but unwieldy, and influenced by the first.

The world pushes us towards a life without anxiety, or at least functioning with it, in an effort to get us to re-engage with the world that piles onto us the conditions that lead to anxiety. You must reduce your anxiety so that you can ride in an airplane 40,000 feet in the sky, go to your horrible job, fight in a war, and on and on. It is about getting back onto that treadmill and having just enough of the edge taken off to continue to do what everyone else does in this civilization that we have built.

The second reason we feel the need to defeat our anxiety is uncontrollable. Our bodies physically feel our anxiety, our angst, our panic, our depression, and our desire to withdraw from life. It must understand why we feel this way. It is a double understanding– one that causes the anxiety and one that seeks to break it.

Remember, as our mind tries to make sense of the world that is around it, the inability to understand it or the inevitably of tragedy and harm that it interprets brings us to a place of unease. There our anxiety is born. But in a turn of irony, it is born into the world, again something to be interpreted. We believe that anxiety is not something that is part of the natural order of ourselves. It must be assimilated into how we view ourselves as part of the world, how we view our body: us in the world.

So it goes like this: we have our thinking, which tries to understand everything. The world presents to us. Our thinking attempts to make sense of it. In making sense of it our thinking is affected. The world presents more of itself. Our thinking attempts to make sense of it but either cannot or is brought to a negative result. We have anxiety. Our mind and body are affected by the anxiety. Our thinking attempts to make sense of our anxiety. More anxiety is caused. And on and on. Meanwhile the world is still coming at us, with its weight, which is simultaneously getting heavy as we are growing tired and weaker.

Our mind is naturally trying to make sense of this. Making sense of it is stopping it.

7.20: Answers

Why do I want to figure out the cause of my anxiety? Why do we always try to beat it?

While originally, it felt like it was just societal pressures and inertia that led down those paths, it seems now, after meditation, that that is only part of the equation. Simply, figuring it out is what we do. We try to make sense of everything presented to us. When anxious thoughts and feelings are presented to us, we cannot help but try to identify the reason, the point, and the source.

The way that we orient that arithmetic, and the way that we point it, is influenced by our experiences, the world around us, society, tradition, and every other external factor that contributes to who we are and how we think. It is automatic—and especially in anxious situations—to a fault. An experience happens, we attempt to process it, conflict arises, and we panic. When I examine that string of thought and reaction,

I look at what I know and what I expect. I examine it because we are constantly examining, like before. We now have, at least, a double examination–that of our natural perceptions, and that of the reaction. There of course may be other layers.

Anxiety is like a bird flying by. Or flying into our window. It is like a rain on our face. Or in our basement. We recognize the cause and effect in all, and we are grasping for it with our anxious thoughts as well. When it is not apparent *or is not even there*, we must treat it differently, we must act differently–from how we treat all feelings, but also from how we function in our automatic thought processes.

In our society and culture, figuring something out and understanding it is equated with beating it. It is not that simple with anxiety and depression. Anxiety is so embedded within our natural state, that simply knowing that it is there and what the cause is does not free us of the consequences. Knowing the status quo does not break the status quo.

7.21: Obligations

We have obligations. We have responsibilities. We have traditions. We have ways that we want to live and ways that we want to be. The truth is, we cannot just do what we want. And we have anxiety about doing those things that we have to do.

So there must be judgment involved. We have to sort out what we actually must do, and what is truly optional. Flying on a plane across the country: optional. You can drive, of course. Working to earn money to pay rent: not optional. You have to have shelter. Of course all of these can have different variables involved, but nonetheless we have to examine and decide.

This is not only a tug-of-war between what we want to do and what our world demands of us. It is also a question of what we want to be. How do we see ourselves and how do we want to be seen? What we do, along with what anxiety we grant and which we diminish, contribute immensely to who we are. Is a person charitable if they do no charity? Are you a lover of nature if you do not go outdoors? You do not have to be any of these things—but you can be these things.

7.22: I Am Having Trouble

I am having trouble writing. I am supposed to be coming out the other side, explaining the way through, offering some type of hope or counter-attack against anxiety. But the truth is: it is not easy. I do not feel great. I am still anxious. Even though I know and believe what I have said, it is still difficult to live it, to feel it, for it to be automatic. My thinking is not a train on the track, that I have pulled the switch on, diverting from some rickety bridge to one of self-determined bliss.

No. I am unsure. I am sad. I am anxious about

tomorrow. Even when I keep reminding myself that these things that fill me with worry are ultimately nothing, and I can focus on, enjoy, and shape the world that I want, I still fret. My eyes still well.

It is hard to think. But I know that mantras are not fixes. Words on a page are not potions. Stress keeps coming, and I am worn down. I hear a voice in my head, "You do not have to believe this. Anxiety is not truth. You may decide," and I believe it. But it is a soft voice. My nerves still reverberate like a tuning fork struck to a sharp note of a minor key.

Here I am, telling you about anxiety, and about pulling back from it. Yet I struggle to back away.

7.23: Matters

It is important that if you learn that nothing matters, you next decide what matters to you. It is important for you to apply meaning to what is meaninglessness.

Meaninglessness, lack of purpose, is adjacent to despair. Hopelessness and the belief that nothing will change, that nothing can get better, is self-fulfilling in the mind. It sounds like just a matter of perspective, but it is more: it is agency.

Push. Apply your own meanings. Create your own worlds. If nothing matters, do not let someone or something else decide what does.

Conclusion

There is a linocut print on my wall of a cloaked man with his arm outstretched, holding back a deluge of water with dark clouds overhead.

With anxiety, we have three options: be overcome by the waves, float with them, or hold them back–reshaping the water.

When the world puts pressure on us, when it tries to shape us, when we move, what do we become?

Made in the USA
Columbia, SC
06 May 2023